CW00916870

John Betjeman

on

Trains

Sir John Betjeman (1906–84), St Pancras Station, 14th November 2007.

John Betjeman

on

Trains

JONATHAN GLANCEY

Methuen

Published by Methuen 2006

7

Methuen
35 Hospital Fields Road
York YO10 4DZ

ISBN: 978-0-413-77612-9

Designed by Bryony Newhouse

Printed in the UK by CPI Group (UK) Ltd, Croydon, CR0 4YY

A CIP catalogue record for this title is available from the British Library

CONTENTS

John Betjeman was a lifelong railway enthusiast. Not, I hasten to say, one who stood, duffel bag, Penguin biscuit and fish-paste sandwiches on murky days at the ends of platforms taking down the numbers of locomotives; but a poet who loved railways from the bottom of his heart.

Railways remain one of the most civilised ways of travelling between any two points in the world, although in Britain, the country that invented them, they have been despised by one car-mad government, with a finger or two in the road-lobby pie, after another. Remarkably, although not particularly pleasant, and certainly far from romantic, our gormlessly privatised, airline-style railways are busier today than they have been for decades. This, though, reflects our increasing desire to get from place to place rather than the attractiveness of trains and railways themselves.

British trains, all too often run by US business school, New Labour-style executives more interested in annual bonuses, personal pension funds, the interests of greedy shareholders, massive state subsidies (far greater than poor old British Railways ever received) and 'customer services facilities' – whatever they may be – are, for the most part, sorry things today. Decked out in colour schemes created by visually illiterate monkeys let loose with boxes of children's crayons, they look quite ridiculous and insult the British landscape. I suppose they look 'chavtastic' to focus group-oriented railway managers, the very thing for their passive 'customers' who are assumed to be morons, willing to pay through the nose for tickets, where once upon a time, and when railway design mattered, they were 'passengers', an altogether more discriminating breed.

Not that our railways were necessarily cherished in earlier days. Far from it. Did Dr Beeching really get to axe all those thousands of miles of railways that would be so useful today? Yes, he did. Did Betjeman really have to fight so very hard to try to save the Euston Arch? Yes, he did. Was such ennobling architecture really swept away on the tides of fundamentalist Modernisation in the early 1960s championed by, of all people, the Tory prime minister Harold Macmillan? Yes, it was. If it hadn't been for Betjeman, and those in his orbit, we would, in all probability, have lost St Pancras and Liverpool Street stations too.

Recently, I lunched with a senior journalist colleague who knows a great deal about architecture and design, yet, nevertheless, suggested that I should give up ever writing about railways. It smacked of childhood, he implied. Do your career no good, old chap. The moment, though, we let our critical attention drift from architecture or railways, some ambitious young executive, council official or jargon-spouting government apparatchik will be plotting the 'regeneration' of some noble work of railway architecture, or trying to close a line, or championing new and unnecessary roads.

Betjeman loved trains not just for themselves, but because they were a wonderful way of travelling through Britain and looking out, without having to drive, at ever-changing townscapes and country-side. He liked the often quixotic histories of Britain's railways, like that of the Great Central which aimed, rather optimistically, for Paris via a Channel tunnel a century ago. And then there was the Somerset and Dorset, hoping to win a slice of transatlantic traffic from the end of its meandering branch line to Burnham-on-Sea.

He liked steam locomotives, of course. It is hard not to be moved by these characterful machines, and he liked the curious byways of Britain's railways. He enjoyed the kiss-me-quick ride along Southend Pier where one of the locomotives that pulls the miniature trains bears his name. He liked to imagine himself working as a station master or booking-office clerk at some obscure rural outpost. I suppose that was the writer in him, dreaming of finding the ideal place to put pen to paper with the occasional enjoyable distraction in the guise of a tank locomotive hissing gently into a platform, all carved woodwork, abundant flower beds and polished brass.

A number of Betjeman's best poems are inspired by railway stations, or journeys to and from them. There is the sad poem, *Baker Street*, where the clockwork comings and goings of Metropolitan Line trains mark the passage of time for a suburban couple looking into their graves. There is the fond satire, *Ruislip Gardens*, which opens with lines set to the clattering rhythm of a rush-hour Central Line tube train:

> Gaily into Ruislip Gardens
> Runs the red electric train
> And, with a thousand tas and pardons
> Daintily alights Elaine

This selection of letters show how railways infused Betjeman's life. They allow him to be impassioned, funny, snobby, satirical and expert. We should all be glad he had that expert knowledge of railways and architecture; far from standing in the way of genuine progress, his love of railways, coupled to his campaigning spirit, means that from autumn 2007 we will be able to travel, at 186mph, from London to Paris from under the great iron and glass train shed of gloriously Gothic St Pancras. Those who take no interest in railways, or their architecture, would have let St Pancras go, and we might well have ridden to the Continent from some soulless, low-ceilinged, fluorescent-lit station set in the irritable bowels of an ill-tempered office block.

Dear Sir John, this book is a letter to say thank you, yours ever, JG.

Holland Park
Central Line,* July 2006

---

* Signal failures and privatised maintenance contracts permitting.

1. 'When some brutal decision is made'

25th August 1954

The Mead
Wantage
Berkshire

Dear Mr Watt,

I have heard from Mr Prosser, the founder of the Railway Development Association, one of whose vice-presidents I am, and he says that he thinks it is a good idea that I should be president of your Society, since the aims of the Railway Development Association and your own are similar. But since hearing from him, I have discussed the matter with my friend Lord Kinross, in whose house I have been staying while in London, and who has had an invitation from you to be president. We both think that the most practical arrangement and the best will be the one which is going to be most useful toward further-ing the objects of the two societies. As we know one another, it seems most sensible that Lord Kinross should be your president and that I should also be a vice-president of the London Area of the Railway Development Association, a position which has been offered to me. In this way Lord Kinross and I will be able to make common cause when some brutal decision is made by British Railways. Lord Kinross is an excellent conversationalist and a wonderfully lucid and vigorous writer, but he asks me to tell you he is no good at making speeches from public platforms. He becomes terrified and tongue-tied. If you want the sort of president who can make public speeches and who is full of knowledge about railways and in sympathy with our aims, he and I both suggest you might care to approach our friend Sir Arthur Elton Bt, of 10 Eldon Grove, NW3. Anyhow, let me know what your Society thinks of the suggestions.

One point, the title of your Society. Ought the word Unremunerative to come out? Doesn't it rather suggest that branchlines always will be unremunerative?

Yours sincerely, John Betjeman

N.W.'s newly formed group was called the Society for the Reinvigoration of Unremunerative Branch Lines in the UK.

Branch lines were being pruned, axed and generally ripped up with gathering speed in the 1950s as the car droned its inexorable way into the English countryside. Betjeman wrote this letter when Winston Churchill was prime minister, just weeks after wartime rationing finally came to an end and the age of Austerity gave way to an unprecedented consumer boom and a prodigious increase in car production. 'Indeed, let us be frank about it', said Harold Macmillan, the prime minister, at a Tory party rally in Bedford in 1957. 'Most of our people have never had it so good. Go around the country, go to the industrial towns, go to the farms and you will see a state of prosperity such as we have never had in my lifetime – nor indeed in the history of this country.'

The end of the decidedly unprosperous rural branch line, however, was firmly in sight. If you look at a railway map of the time, you will be astonished to see that almost any English village worth its beer, thatch or medieval church, could be reached by train. Most of these were still steam-hauled. Locomotives might well be Victorian, sauntering along winding tracks with perhaps just one coach, all horsehair-stuffed seats, cart-spring suspension and framed views of seaside resorts gracing compartment walls, and a milk wagon in tow. Others were deceptively racy. The

A class 14xx Tank, No. 1439 posing with its crew. *Transport Treasury*

tiny former Great Western Railway 14xx class 0–4–2 tank locomotives, for example, that looked Victorian but which dated from as recently as 1936, could spin their single push-pull maroon 'autocoaches' along Gloucestershire valleys at speeds of up to 80mph and more, and did so until well into 1964.

All such branch line adventures were a delight to train buffs. JB had many favourites, but was typically keen on the curious former Great Eastern Railway branch that ran through rural Essex between Epping and Ongar. This bucolic line was to become a most unlikely electric outpost of London Transport's Central Line when the last steam trains ran in 1957.

Blake Hall station, looking towards Ongar, 26th January 1957.
L R Freeman / Transport Treasury

Betjeman once said that his ideal job would have been station master at Blake Hall, a pretty little red brick station (now a private residence) along a line that might have been two hundred miles from the City of London in the 1950s. The branch was closed in 1994. It has been partly, and, sporadically, re-opened by enthusiasts since.

Saving the branch lines was always going to be difficult because they tended to lose money like steam through the safety-valves of a tank engine. Who wanted to walk to a lonely railway station bearing the name of their village hidden somewhere among willow-herb and hollyhocks perhaps three or four miles away, when

A class F5 Tank, No. 67193 departing from Epping, 26th January 1957.
L R Freeman / Transport Treasury

a bright new Austin or Morris, bought on the 'never never' could take them from cottage door to city shops at a steady 50mph? Charles Crichton's popular Ealing Comedy, *The Titfield Thunderbolt*, released in 1953 had done a good job romanticising a former Great Western branch line (the Limpley Stoke to Camerton branch, closed 1951) threatened by a seedy bus company run by a Gor' blimey spiv played by Sid James. Buses were seen as common compared with trains, but even they, with their low overhead costs, were no match for the lures of the common-as-axle-grease private car.

In this letter, Betjeman wisely advises Watt to drop the word 'Unremunerative' from the unhappily negative and decidedly clumsy title of his Society for the Reinvigoration of Unremunerative Branch Lines' – yet these picturesque and useful railways still went. However, not even Betjeman at his most melancholy could have imagined the destruction of branch lines yet to come. The single worst year for unremunerative branch lines was 1964 when Dr Richard Beeching (1913–85), the new chairman of British Railways, wielded his infamous 'axe' with full force. In that year alone, Britain lost 1,058 railway miles.

Beeching was appointed in 1961 by Ernest Marples, Harold Macmillan's Minister of Transport, who was a former director of a major road construction company and liked to say that railways were a relic of our Victorian past. The new chairman set to work with a vengeance. The 'Beeching Plan' resulted in the closure of a third of Britain's 18,000-mile railway network. At the time of Betjeman's letter to Watt, this figure had been 21,000 route miles. Those villages losing their trains were promised 'bustitution'. In reality, this seedy-sounding practice rarely caught on. The trains went. Replacement bus services were few and far between. Of lines kept open, 2,128 stations were to be closed. In future, main-line trains would only stop at major towns. For many people, the car was to be the only option.

None of this was enough for Beeching. In 1965, he published a barking mad follow-up to his infamous report of two years earlier. This proposed that all railways other than Inter City and key commuter lines serving major cities should close, cutting the system to just 7,000 miles. There were to be no railways at all in Betjeman's beloved Cornwall, nor in neighbouring Devon. The recommendations were rejected by Harold Wilson's Labour government. Beeching resigned. The nation that invented the railway breathed a collective sigh of relief. And, yet, the 'axe' was to fall again, repeatedly, in the late Sixties and into the Seventies; 1974 was the first year, post-Beeching, that no lines were closed.

It has not all been doom and gloom, far from it. The love of railways encouraged by Betjeman and others, as well as the environmental movement, and sheer common sense, had led to the re-opening of many lines and stations since the early 1980s. The Coventry to Nuneaton line re-opened in 1988. Mansfield, the largest town in England without a railway at the time, was reconnected to Worksop and Nottingham in the early 1990s. The Ebbw Vale branch in South Wales re-opens this year.

Meanwhile, the spirit and flavour of many favourite old branch lines has been recreated by preservation societies. Beginning with the Bluebell Railway, running vintage trains between Sheffield Park and Horsted Keynes in mid-Sussex in 1960, just two years after the line's closure, steam trains have returned to a host of branch lines the length and breadth of Britain.

In his poem *Dilton Marsh Halt* (a rudimentary station, still open, between Warminster and Westbury), JB prophesised that 'Steam trains will return.' They have. This little station is a fine spot to watch mighty main-line steam locomotives – Merchant Navys, Kings, Princess Coronations – thunder by on main-line specials today.

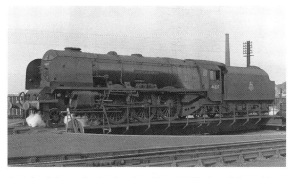

A mighty Princess Coronation class, No. 46227 *Duchess of Devonshire* at Polmadie, 18th May 1953. *J Robertson / Transport Treasury*

A Merchant Navy class (later rebuilt) No. 35001 *Channel Packet* at Exeter Central, August 1955. *L R Freeman/Transport Treasury*

A rebuilt Merchant Navy class No. 35023 *Holland-Afrika Line* at Exmouth Junction shed, August 1957. *W Hermiston/Transport Treasury*

JB's letter of 1954 tells us much about the way in which wealthy and otherwise well-connected enthusiasts played their part in those early days of branch line preservation. Betjeman recommends a baronet, Sir Arthur Elton (1906–73), the documentary film maker, and a peer, Lord Kinross (1904–76), author and journalist, to help Watt in his mission to save Britain's small railways. Sir Arthur had been a schoolfriend of JB. In the 1930s he worked as a producer and director with John Grierson's celebrated GPO Film Unit. Among the famous documentaries they made was *Night Mail* (1936) which featured the LMS Royal Scot 4–6–0 *Seaforth Highlander* galloping down from Shap at the head of the famous West Coast Postal from Euston to Glasgow, a stirring score by Benjamin Britten and a rattlingly good railway poem by W H Auden: 'This is the Night Mail crossing the border / Bringing the cheque and the postal order …'. Elton worked, as did JB for a spell, for the Ministry of Information during the Second World War, and, afterwards, became head of production for Shell Films. JB wrote three of the Shell Guides to English counties. Elton left a collection of some 5,000 books and documents relating to Britain's early industrial development, including its railways, to the Ironbridge Museum, Shropshire.

Lord Kinross, or Patrick Balfour, 3rd Baron Kinross

Rebuilt Royal Scot class, No. 46108 *Seaforth Highlander*, at Carstairs. Unmodified, this locomotive starred in the 1936 film documentary, *Night Mail*. *M Robertson/Transport Treasury*

was an old friend of Betjeman's from his Oxford University days. A well-connected socialite, he is best known for his enduring history of modern Turkey, *Ataturk: The Rebirth of a Nation* (1964).

As for the Society for the Reinvigoration of Unremunerative Branch Lines in the UK (Watt appears not to have taken JB's advice to drop the 'Unremunerative'), this soldiered on into the mid-1960s. It even got a mention in *Time* magazine in 1962 when a US journalist reporting on the Beeching effect, noted that 'Hundreds of Englishmen exist for the sole purpose of keeping branch lines running, raising cash to rent doomed

Horsted Keynes (now on the Bluebell line.) A class I3 No. 32088 with the Oxted to Brighton service, 9th September 1950.
R C Riley/Transport Treasury

sections from Railway Boss Beeching, making weekend pilgrimages to such officially abandoned routes as the Bluebell ('Nowhere to Nowhere') loop in Sussex. Despite a petition signed by 25,000 rail buffs, the Society for the Reinvigoration of Unremunerative Branch Lines in the United Kingdom (SRUBLUK) failed to keep open the scenic reach between Westerham and Dunton Green in Kent last October.'

Today, though, the fight put up by the likes of Watt, Kinross, Elton and JB, among very many others, has won through. Branch lines have been reopening, while steam trains puff contentedly along many of them.

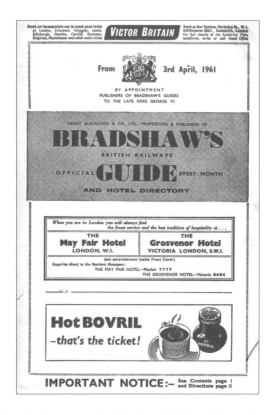

Above: The front cover of Bradshaw's British Rail Guide for April 1961. Publication ceased in June 1961. *Network Rail*

Overleaf: Typical pages from Bradshaw's showing the trains that JB used to meet John Arlott. *Network Rail*

2. 'The 8.32 from Alresford'

TO JOHN ARLOTT

26th March 1965

43 Cloth Fair
London EC1

My dear John,

You mistake my influence which is negligible, but I know what you mean and I so agree about the disruption of little country towns by blind, statistic-minded do-gooders that I must do all I can to get to you. On the other hand, I must get back on the same night, as I have a very early, extremely important meeting on the same subject the next morning. So far as I can see, the only possible trains are the 4.35 ex Waterloo arriving Winchester 5.48, which would give me a little time to have a look round the town, and I would have to catch the 8.32 back from Alresford, if that were possible, as the 10.03 from that station doesn't get back until 11.46 and I am very hard pressed. If I find, as is all too likely, that I really can't manage it, I will ring you up on Monday and send you instead a letter along lines we could discuss on the

LONDON, BASINGSTOKE, SOUTHAMPTON, LYMINGTON, BOURNEMOUTH, SWANAGE and WEYMOUTH

Week Days

Table 32—continued   Down

B Applies until 17th September, 1960 and again commencing 20th May, 1961

5 38 pm from Portsmouth and Southsea (Table 54)

5 5 pm from Alton (Table 53)

Mondays to Fridays

To Brockenhurst (Table 34)

Restaurant Car Waterloo to Bournemouth

THE ROYAL WESSEX

Through Carriages to Swanage

5 8 pm from Portsmouth and Southsea (Table 54)

Mondays to Fridays

Via Alton (Table 53)

To Southampton Terminus

Mondays to Fridays

Via Alton (Table 53)

Fridays only

Saturdays only

Arr St. Denys 5 45 pm

5 3 pm from Portsmouth and Southsea to Salisbury (Table 54)

Mondays to Fridays

To Bournemouth West Via Ringwood (Table 34)

Restaurant Car Train from York

Saturdays only

Until 29th Oct., 1960 and again commencing 6th May, 1961

Mondays to Fridays

Restaurant Car Train from York

Until 28th Oct., 1960 and again commencing 1st May, 1961

Mondays to Fridays

5 4 pm from Romsey (Table 54)

4 37 pm from Portsmouth and Southsea (Table 54)

Stop

Arr Poole 7 1 pm

To Templecombe (Table 36)

b 2 minutes later 31st October, 1960 to 29th April, 1961

31st October, 1960 to 29th April, 1961

Until 29th Oct., 1960 and again commencing 1st May, 1961

Mondays to Fridays

Mondays to Fridays

To Wimborne (Table 34)

To Andover Junction (Table 54)

Restaurant Car Waterloo to Bournemouth

Buffet Car

Stop

B Applies until 17th September, 1960 and again commencing 20th May, 1961

Via Alton (Table 53)

To Portsmouth and Southsea (Table 54)

4 3 pm from Portsmouth and Southsea to Salisbury (Table 54)

4 13 pm from Romsey (SX) 3 36 pm from Andover Junction (SO) (Table 54)

LONDON Waterloo
Surbiton
Woking 77
Weybridge
Farnborough
Fleet
Winchfield
Hook

Basingstoke
Micheldever
Winchester City
Shawford

Eastleigh
Swaything
St. Denys
Northam

Southampton Terminus

Southampton Central
Millbrook
Redbridge
Lyndhurst Road
Beaulieu Road

Brockenhurst

Lymington Town
Lymington Pier
Yarmouth Slipway

New Milton
Hinton Admiral
Christchurch
Pokesdown
Boscombe

Bournemouth Central

Bournemouth West
Branksome
Parkstone
Poole
Hamworthy Junction
Wareham
Wool
Moreton
Dorchester South
Upwey and Broadway
Weymouth

Swanage
Corfe Castle
Wareham

16

Table 53 LONDON, ALTON, ALRESFORD, EASTLEIGH and SOUTHAMPTON

Down — Week Days

Miles		am	am	am	am	am	am	pm	pm	pm	pm	SO	SX	SO	SX	SO	pm	pm	pm	pm
	LONDON Waterloo 77 .. dep	5	256	257	258	259	27	1027	1227	1227	272	273	273	274	274	475	275	276	146	277	278	57
—	Alton .... dep	7	118	08	51	9	53	1053	1153	1253	532	533	534	535	5	536	6	496	537	327	538	53	1025
5½	Medstead and Four Marks ,,	7	208	99	010	210	212	21	22	23	24	25	25	146	26	146	587	274	538	29	7	1034
54½	Ropley .... ,,	7	248	139	410	610	612	61	62	63	64	65	65	66	66	387	27	67	508	69	6	1038
57	Alresford .... ,,	7	308	239	810	1010	1012	102	102	103	104	105	105	106	1068	7	107	549	109	101	941
60½	Itchen Abbas ...... ,,	7	398	289	1310	511	1512	152	152	153	154	155	33	156	33	7	157	598	159	7	1043
65	Winchester City ... ,,	7	488	389	2210	2411	2412	242	242	243	244	245	245	456	246	47	7	248	189	249	241	1057
69	Shawford .... ,,	7	538	439	27	19	9	19	25	47	8	18	79	11	37
72½	Eastleigh .... ,,	7	598	499	3510	1034	1234	1234	342	3363	344	3405	3408	706	346	567	348	198	349	3611
75	Swaythling .... ,,	8	78	569	4310	3810	4210	4212	422	433	42	5474	586	427	2	418	278	429	4411	16
76½ St. Denys .... ,,	8	78	569	4310	4210	1042	1042	422	433	42	547	586	427	2	418	278	429	4411	16
77	Northam .... ,,	8	98	599	4510	4410	1044	1244	442	493	47	5	526	136	477	7	468	328	479	49
78½ Southampton Terminus . arr	129	29	4810	4710	4710	4712	472	493	47	5	526	136	477	7	468	328	479	49
78½ Southampton Central ... ,,																				1121

Down — Sundays

		am	am		am	am		am	am		pm	pm		pm	pm		pm	pm		pm	pm	pm
	LONDON Waterloo 77 .. dep	7	57		8	57	8	57	9	57		1057	1157		1257	57		2	573	57		4	575	57	..	6	57	7	57	8	57
	Alton .... dep	8	259	25		1025	1125		1225	25		1	253	25		25	..	6	257	25		8	25	9	2610	26
	Medstead and Four Marks ,,	8	349	34		1034	1134		1234	34		2	343	34		34	4	345	34		6	347	34		8	34	9	3510	35
	Ropley .... ,,	8	389	38		1038	1138		1238	38		2	383	38		38	4	385	38		6	387	38		8	38	9	3910	39
	Alresford .... ,,	8	429	42		1042	1142		1242	42		2	423	42		42	4	425	42		6	427	42		8	42	9	4310	43
	Winchester City ... ,,	8	559	55		1055	1155		1254	55		2	563	55		55	4	555	55		6	557	55		8	55	9	5710	58
	Shawford .... ,,	9	010	0		11	012	0		0		10	0		3	4		6	06	0		7	0		9	0
	Eastleigh .... ,,	9	610	6		1118	12	6		72	6		3	74	6		6	66	6	7	68	6		9	610	1011	17
	Swaythling .... ,,	9	1010	10		1112	1210		110	10		3	104	10		10	7	108	10		9	1010	1411	11
	St. Denys .... ,,	9	1410	14		1116	1214		152	14		3	154	14		5	146	14	7	148	14		9	1410	1811	15
	Northam .... ,,																						
	Southampton Terminus . arr																						
	Southampton Central ... ,,	9	1910	19		1121	1219		1	202	19		3	191	19		19	7	199	19		9	1910	2311	20

Up — Week Days

Miles		am	am	am	am	am	am	pm		pm	pm	SX	SO	SX	SO	SX		pm	pm	pm
	Southampton Central ...... dep																			
	Southampton Terminus .. ,,	5	536	537	398	539	1053	1153	1253		1	552	533	534	464	535	465	53		6	537	519	24
1	Northam .... ,,	5	596	557	418	559	559	1055	1155	1255		572	553	554	484	555	485	55		6	557	539	26
3	St. Denys .... ,,	6	586	587	468	589	58	1058	1158	1258		2	003	583	584	514	585	515	58		6	587	569	29
5	Swaythling .... ,,	6	607	67	509	110	611	612	6		2	305	04	145	455	156		7	18	19	32
9	Eastleigh .... ,,	6	677	67	539	69	612	612	6		2	83	64	645	975	65	596	6		7	88	89	34
5	Shawford .... ,,	6	127	127	599	12													75X12		19	37
12½ Winchester City ...... ,,	6	287	188	77	18	1018	1118	1218	18		2	183	184	185	115	186	156	18		7	188	189	49
17	Itchen Abbas .... ,,	6	377	268	159	26	1026	1126	1226	26		2	263	264	265	195	266	266	26		7	268	269	57
21½ Alresford .... ,,	6	447	328	229	32	1032	1132	1232	32		2	323	324	325	265	326	266	32		7	328	329	10	3
24	Ropley .... ,,	6	527	377	279	37	1037	1137	1237	37		2	373	374	375	315	316	376	37		7	378	379	10
27	Medstead and Four Marks ,,	6	587	448	349	44	1044	1144	1244	44		2	443	444	445	385	446	386	44		7	448	449	10
31½ Alton .... arr	7	78	508	409	50	1050	1150	1250	50		2	503	504	505	465	506	456	507	29		7	508	501021
78½ LONDON Waterloo 77 .. arr	8	409	1099	57	1118	1218	162	1673	16		4	165z	7161187	167	168	168	16	..	9	161016	1146

Up — Sundays

		am	am	am	am	am	am	pm		pm	pm		B	pm	pm	pm	pm
	Southampton Central .... dep	7	259	25		9	251025		1125	1225		1	253	25		4	255	25		6	257	25		pm	pm
	Southampton Terminus .. ,,																			
	Northam .... ,,																			
	St. Denys .... ,,	7	309	30		9	301030		1130	1230		1	303	30		4	305	30		6	307	30		9	30
	Swaythling .... ,,	7	349	34		9	341034		1134	1234		1	343	343	34		4	345	34		6	307	34		9	349	34
	Eastleigh .... ,,	7	389	38		9	381038		1138	1238		1	383	383	38		4	385	38		6	307	38		9	389	38
	Shawford .... ,,	7	449	44		9	441044		1144	1244		1	443	44		4	445	44		6	447	44		9	449	44
	Winchester City ...... ,,	7	509	50		9	501050		1150	1250		1	503	50		4	505	50		6	507	50		9	509	50
	Itchen Abbas .... ,,																			
	Alresford .... ,,	8			10	311		231			2	323	323	2		5	8				8	310
	Ropley .... ,,	8			10	71		281			2	83	83	82		5	8				8	710
	Medstead and Four Marks ,,	8	159	15		1015	111		151			2	153	154	152		5	152	15		8	210
	Alton .... arr	8	219	21		1021	1121		1221	21		2	213	214	21		5	216	21		7	218	21		9	211021
	LONDON Waterloo 77 ... arr	9	461046		1146	1246		1	462	46		4	465	46		6	487	46		8	469	47		1046	1146

A Arr 11 minutes earlier.   a Arr 9 16 am on Saturdays.   B 4 43 pm from Fawley.   h Arr 10 16 am on Saturdays.
c Arr 1 12 pm on Saturdays.   d Arr 4 minutes earlier.   e Arr 2 12 pm on Saturdays.   F Arr 2 minutes earlier.
f Arr 6 16 pm on Saturdays.   g Arr 5 17 pm on Saturdays.   R To Portsmouth and Southsea (arr 5 17 pm, Table 54).
Arr Eastleigh 4 35 pm   L Arr 3 minutes earlier.   SO Saturdays only.   SX or SX Mondays to Fridays.
                          T Arr 7 minutes earlier.   X Arr 5 minutes earlier.   † Arrival

For OTHER TRAINS between London and Southampton, see Table 32
For COMPLETE SERVICE between Winchester and Southampton, see Table 32

telephone. It was lovely seeing you and Valerie and that large-eyed Robert and drinking that delicious claret and burgundy. Keep heart. Don't exercise the will too much, and share your sadness with others. It helps.

Yours, JB

Alresford station, looking towards London, 5th October 1957.
L R Freeman / Transport Treasury

For forty-six years John Arlott (1914–91) was the 'Voice of Cricket'. His lovely Hampshire burr, an accent rarely heard in the broadcast media today, was for millions of people, the 'sound of summer', of leather-against-willow, of cricketers who still wore 'whites' rather than today's baseball caps and Day-Glo rap-artist jump-suits plastered in corporate logos, and of a seemingly unchanging England. Of course, England, and especially small towns much like his own Alresford (pronounced Allsford) in the heart of Hampshire were changing quickly in the mid-1960s when the BBC radio broadcaster asked if JB would come down on the train from Waterloo to attend a local planning meeting to help fight churlishly modern plans to mess up the town. Modernisation was very much in the air at the time.

This was the era of Harold Wilson's 'white hot technology', when steam trains were being scrapped as fast as anyone with a spare blow torch could cut them up, new motorways were scarring the landscape and cheap and cheerless new concrete housing estates and shopping centres were being built wherever, and whenever, some ambitious local authority had the chance of demolishing our Georgian and Victorian inheritance and getting away with it. JB's poem, *Executive*, sums up the mood of the times:

I do some mild developing. The sort of place I need
Is a quiet country town that's rather gone to seed.
A luncheon and a drink or two, a little savoire faire –
I fix the Planning Officer, The Town Clerk and the Mayor.

And if some preservationist attempts to interfere
A 'dangerous stucture' notice from the Borough Engineer
Will settle any buildings that are standing in our way –
The modern style, sir, with respect, has really come to stay.

'I must say', Arlott had written JB on 23rd March, 'that I believe your very presence would make the planners stop and think – and wonder whether they can, in fact, get away with all these small town changes by default or, at least, without any real stir.' Betjeman was clearly hard-pressed for time that week, but, nevertheless, managed a fleeting evening trip down from Waterloo and back. Did his presence in Alresford make a difference? Perhaps it did. Today, change to many such small towns is faster and more painful than ever, and yet Alresford remains, for the most part, an enchanting Georgian market town, complete with the kind of second hand bookshops, tea rooms and antique shops that have been replaced by estate agents, charity shops and video stores that dominate the high streets of all too many small English market towns today.

Arlott himself lived at The Old Sun, East Street, a former eighteenth-century inn that once refreshed sheep drovers. He would have been well aware that the world is always changing even in rural Hampshire. Alresford itself, laid out in medieval times by Bishop de Lucy, was all but destroyed by fire in the seventeenth century and rebuilt. In 1943, it was very nearly destroyed again by a USAAF B-17 Flying Fortress bomber that, fully armed, dived out of control towards the town centre. The crew bailed out, except for the pilot who saved the day, by steering the aircraft towards fields, and heroically jumping to safety at only the very last possible moment.

Betjeman rode to Winchester on the '4.35 ex Waterloo'. This would have been a delightful journey for the poet as, in spring 1965, express and semi-fast trains along the former London & South Western Railway main line from Waterloo to Southampton via Winchester were still steam-hauled. Long rakes of smooth-sided 'malachite' green coaches designed by Oliver Snell Bulleid, the last Chief Mechanical Engineer of the Southern Railway, were raced along behind stirring Bulleid Pacifics of the West Country, Battle of Britain and Merchant Navy classes. Designed and built during and just after the Second World War, and rebuilt as late as 1961, these were the most

Battle of Britain class No. 34084 *253 Squadron* at Waterloo 1963.
A H Roscoe/Transport Treasury

A Merchant Navy class (later rebuilt) No. 35007 *Aberdeen Commonwealth* on the Honiton incline, 3rd August 1955. *J Robertson/Transport Treasury*

modern passenger steam locomotives running on British Railways, and this was the last steam main line in and out of London. The last ran in July 1967 when the line from Waterloo to Southampton and Bournemouth was finally electrified. Waterloo is where, too, of course, the Betjemann family (with a double 'n' until the First World War) had steamed on its way to its annual summer holiday in Cornwall. JB was particularly fond of these 'South Western' memories.

Those last couple of years of Waterloo steam were highly spirited. Although the outward appearance of these handsome, powerful locomotives was often unkempt, and most had lost their numberplates and

A rebuilt West Country class No. 34040 *Crewkerne* at Southampton en route from Bournemouth to Waterloo, September 1962. *A H Roscoe/ Transport Treasury*

nameplates, their drivers revelled in having 'one last go' at travelling as fast as possible. Speeds of 100mph and more became almost commonplace as the Bulleid Pacifics sprinted between Basingstoke, where Arlott was born, and Woking, along past the town's pretty Victorian mosque, on their way up to Waterloo.

Although JB rode down on the fast main line to Winchester, where, presumably, Arlott would have picked him up by car, he returned direct from Alresford along the delightful 'Watercress Line' via Alton to Waterloo. Although slower, trains over this line, closed soon after the end of Southern steam, enjoyed a glorious ride up, through and over some of the most unspoilt rural scenery so close to London. From Alresford, trains thundered up the steep grade to Medstead & Four Marks, one of the highest stations in southern England, before scooting down to Alton. Railwaymen and enthusiasts alike described this section of the journey as going 'over the Alps'.

Happily, you can still ride over 'the Alps' in smooth-sided 'malachite' green Bulleid coaches behind superb Brunswick green Bulleid Pacifics today. A section of the 'Watercress Line' runs between Alton, where it connects with privatised and garishly painted Southern electrics for Waterloo, and Alresford. Remarkably, the countryside has changed very little since JB rode this way to meet John Arlott a little over forty years ago. With luck, the 'Watercress Line' might reach Winchester again, although many railway preservation societies are used to having such luck dashed by pro-car local authorities who wilfully allow developments of gimcrack 'executive' housing estates across old railway trackbeds in a bid to stop trains from running over them again. The line is charged with steam, beauty and more than a little poetry today.

Arlott wrote poetry, too, and was famous for his poetic, and often bibulous, turns of phrase on the radio. When Clive Lloyd, the celebrated West Indian

Part of Waterloo station in April 1963. Today it is a modern twenty-first century terminal. *B H Fletcher/Transport Treasury*

batsman sent a ball flying into the Mound Stand at Lord's cricket ground in 1975, Arlott described the action as 'the stroke of a man knocking a thistle top off with a walking stick.' Arlott and Betjeman went back a long way. JB had liked poems published by Arlott during the Second World War, and in 1945 he used his influence to land him the job of poetry producer for the BBC World Service's Eastern Service. The next year, Arlott was asked to cover England's cricketing tour of India, and that was that, as far as BBC Radio cricket commentary was concerned, until the Hampshireman's last broadcast in 1980.

Valerie, in JB's letter, was Arlott's wife. The last sentence refers to the death of James, their son, who was killed after driving his MG into the back of a slowly moving lorry that had just turned out from a service station on the A31 in the early hours of New Year's Day, 1965. Arlott never got over the loss.

3. 'The Somerset and Dorset Railway'

TO BRIAN JOHNSON

23rd September 1962

Treen
Trebetherick
Wadebridge

Dear Mr Johnson

I have now read the *History of the S[omerset] and D[orset Railway]*. As you probably gathered from it, the line from Evercreech to Highbridge was opened in 1854 and extended to Burnham in 1858. It was the Somerset Central Line that merged with the Dorset Central to become the S and D. When Queen Square (now Green Park) Bath opened in 1870, where the head offices of the S and D were, the line from Bath to Bournemouth became the main line and the poor old Evercreech–Highbridge line became a branch. It was originally broad gauge as the old Somerset Central was friendly with G[reat] W[estern] R[ailway] which was already at Highbridge. The GWR station at Highbridge is an original Bristol and Exeter line station of the 1840s, nearly twenty years older than the S and D; part of the battle for the Broad Gauge of the line to Burnham on Sea was broad gauge. The station at Burnham was not called Burnham on Sea until 1923. The S and D hoped that Highbridge would be its cargo port for S[outh] Wales and Burnham its passenger and *light* cargo port. All these hopes died when the S and D concentrated on linking Bournemouth with Birmingham and the Midlands via Bath. I don't think any of this is filmic but it is certainly interesting historically. What we looked at at Highbridge was blasted hopes – as you said, 'The Sad Road to the Sea' – a sad road for goods as well as passengers.

So we should think of that 1.15 we caught from Evercreech in September 1962 as the last effort to link the south coast of England with the Welsh collieries, an effort which started over a century ago. This gives you a good visual excuse for goods sequences, for this original part of what became the S and D, was intended to be every bit as important as, say, the London Tilbury and Southend or the London and Blackwall or the L[ondon] and N[orth] W[estern] to your own Liverpool and Holyhead. And no doubt the S and D directors thought, when they built their stations alone on Sedgemoor – Shapwick, Bason Bridge and the like – that there would grow up around them thriving communities as there have grown up around the stations on non-important main lines –

hence the 'Railway Hotel' we saw outside one of the stations on the south side of the line and the S and D Hotel at Burnham. Highbridge was to be another Cardiff. But it failed. The standard gauge of what became the main line of the S and D and the traffic from the Midlands did in the Highbridge and S[outh] Wales experiment.

What became of the freight? All that was to go by sea across to Wales and come from Wales to Somerset and the south coast is a ghost among those empty trucks at Highbridge Harbour. Even the engine works, to be another Crewe or Swindon, are a ghost. Three small tank engines (one is figure 28 in the Barrie and Clinker's book-let) were the only engines built there, but there must have been many buckets of Prussian blue paint and white paint and much gold leaf and many rich transfers for the coats of arms of the splendid S and D line, which I can just remember.

What became of the passengers? The paddle steam-ers failed (figure 3 in Barrie and Clinker) like the extension beyond Burnham station to the jetty which is no longer there – I remember you noticed the gradient mark right at the end of the line pointing only a few feet to the buffers. And now the swell hotel 'the Queens' contains Birmingham people who come by car, not by S and D, and probably no Cardiff people at all.

Having regard to these grandiose plans, I fancy we

should introduce the film with a series of stills (captions I think you call them) of S and D engines, steamships, posters and time tables, and ending on the façade and interior of Bath Green Park so as to give one a chance of telling the S and D story. The only decent bit of writing in Barrie and Clinker is on page 28:

> Under-engined trains crawled hesitantly up the gruelling Mendip grades [and here we might have some shots in still form of trains on the more obviously picturesque parts of the line around Shepton] and went bucketing down the reverse slopes at hell-for-leather speeds to make up time, with the rattletrap coaches cavorting on the primitive, ill-ballasted track … Long delays and complex shunts were the order of the day at the crossing stations, between which trains moved spasmodically on the telegraphed instructions of a functionary known as 'the Crossing Agent', who from his office in Bath endeavoured to play a nightmare game of blind man's chess – with an odd piece or two inexplicably missing ('left Evercreech Junction two hours ago, not yet showed up at Shepton').

And then from the grandeur of Green Park we could switch suddenly to live contrast in the country at Evercreech Junction and follow the line from there to Burnham with the end you had in view.

Quite how you are going to mix goods and passenger along this enchanting track I do not know. A lot will depend on what sort of shots you have and which have the most visual appeal. Personally, I think they could be intermixed and there would be no harm in using the passenger train as the main theme and stopping, where there are good shots, and putting them in.

Though the Evercreech–Highbridge line was started with such high hopes, we don't want to give the impression that it is now a useless anomaly. It occurs to me while writing this, that before we set off in the train from Evercreech you might care to show the line from the point of view of a motorist – the stations like Shapwick seemingly so lonely and pointless in their flat waste when seen from the road (and incidentally miles from the villages after which they were named), so that when we come to travel on the line it has obvious use and significance and seems quite different. I remember how amazed I was to see Shapwick station when motoring over Sedgemoor a few months ago and how different it seemed when travelling through it on Friday.

Anyhow this is how I see the order of the film:

History and Posters of S and D
Evercreech and Country Stations Goods and Passenger Stuff
Highbridge Works

Highbridge Harbour and Crossing of GWR thereto
Burnham Station
Burnham End of Line and Short

I hope you will be able to read all this. It is partly to remind me as much as you of what I saw and to thank you for so pleasant a time. It will also remind me, when the time comes for commentary, of my impressions. You had Burnham impressions down on the tape. Best wishes to you and to all my Bristol BBC friends.

Yours, John Betjeman

I return the books herewith. JB

B.J. seems to have been working for the BBC in Bristol at that time and was involved with JB's film which was eventually broadcast on 21 February 1964.

In March 2006, a former Somerset and Dorset Joint Railway locomotive, No. 89, a 7F 2–8–0 freight locomotive designed by James Clayton of the Midland Railway, Derby, and built at Doncaster by Robert Stephenson & Hawthorne in 1925, sat proudly, for the first time in forty-two years, under the great glass canopy of Bath Green Park Station. The moment was very special. The Somerset and Dorset, one of the most picturesque main lines in England, had closed in March 1966, and its grandest station, Bath Green Park, had been turned into a branch of the supermarket chain, Sainsbury's. Although Sainsbury's has looked

Johnson 0–4–4T, No. 58072, on loan from Highbridge leaving Bath for Binegar, 25th April 1955. *The Ivo Peters Collection*

33

The imposing *Evening Star*, a 9F 2–10–0, No. 92220 standing in Bath Green Station en route for Bournemouth, 12th September 1963. *The Ivo Peters Collection*

after the former Victorian station well, its opulent train shed has, for many years, been nothing more than a car park where people load up with more suavely packaged food than they will ever need, or wish, to eat.

Cars, roads and supermarket culture had done for the old S&D. It was a wonder then, in 2006, to see an S&D locomotive back where it rightly belonged, and Bath Green Park looking like a railway station once more. An attempt is being made today to revive a stretch of the S&D at Midsomer Norton, yet it is extremely unlikely that this wonderfully tortuous line over the Mendips, via Evercreech Junction and

On a bright Saturday afternoon, No. 76027 leaves Evercreech Junction on the S & D line for Bournemouth, 12th March 1955. *The Ivo Peters Collection*

Templecombe, between Bath and Bournemouth, will ever regain anything like its former glory. Luckily, the railway as Betjeman would have known it when he came here to film with BBC Bristol in 1962 was being filmed, assiduously, by the enthusiast and photographer, Ivo Peters. His films of the S&D in the 1960s are a joy to watch today. It seems almost impossible that such a line should have continued to exist in Harold Wilson's white hot technological age. It steamed – it was never dieselised, much less modernised – to the end of its bucolic, semaphore-signalled days.

The S&D had always been an extraordinary line,

Class 2P No. 40568 heads SR Pacific No. 34107 *Blandford Forum* down the bank towards Midsomer Norton with the *Pines Express*, 7th June 1958. *The Ivo Peters Collection*

A local train from Bath to Shepton Mallet. An S & D 4F 0–6–0, No. 44560 crossing Charlton Viaduct with the Mendips behind, 7th September 1963. *The Ivo Peters Collection*

carrying holiday passenger traffic through from the North and the Midlands, from 1874, to the Dorset coast over hills that would have given Swiss railway engineers pause for thought. Passenger trains, like the famous *Pines Express*, were double-headed, usually with a 7F 2–8–0 adding the necessary hill-climbing muscle, over the Mendips. These trains made a slow, if life-enhancing sight and sound. It was at the end of British Railways' Summer timetable of 1962, when JB was in correspondence with Brian Johnson of BBC Bristol, that the *Pines Express*, the S&D's principal passenger train, was diverted away from Bath and the Mendips, to a new route via Oxford and Basingstoke: the decline and fall of this most romantic railway had been set and sealed.

Typically, JB wanted to concentrate filming with the BBC on the S&D's withered arm, the line that meandered from Evercreech Junction to Highbridge and Burnham-on-Sea. Passenger trains had been withdrawn from the branch on September 8th 1962, and goods trains ceased to run the following May. JB's film was to be a memorial to a line that once had ambitions to connect not just Bath to Bournemouth, but Somerset to South Wales and London to the eastern seaboard of the United States, via Highbridge and Burnham. This kind of Victorian vainglory was very attractive to Betjeman. Just as he liked the story of Sir Edward Watkin, chairman of the Great Central Railway, who planned to run trains from Manchester to Paris via Marylebone and his proposed Channel Tunnel, and who went so far as to raise the first stage of an Eiffel Tower lookalike alongside his main line to London at Wembley, so he enjoyed the doomed attempt by the S&D to become an important international transport link.

The harbour at Highbridge has long silted up, and could never berth ships bound for the Atlantic and America let along the coal fields north of Cardiff, once easily reached from here by tramp steamer. Betjeman delighted in the grandiose engine shed at Highbridge. It was, as he says, to have been another 'Crewe or Swindon', although the few British Railway Standard class tank locomotives that simmered in the shed here in 1962 were not exactly the mighty 'Kings' of Swindon, nor the 'Princess Coronations' of Crewe. They looked like scruffy 1950s' schoolboys dressed in jumpers several sizes too big.

If the S&D had succeeded, Highbridge motive power depot – the name given to major engine sheds

Highbridge station looking towards Bristol, 20th August 1960.
L R Freeman / Transport Treasury

– would have been choc-a-bloc with powerful steam locomotives finished in the S&D's richly handsome livery of Prussian blue, red and white. Most of the locomotives that worked the line from the 1920s to the 1960s were, however, painted black. Recently, one of the two happily preserved and normally black S&D 7F 2–8–0s has been turned out in the very same Prussian blue that, in this letter to Brian Johnson, JB says he can 'just remember'. It is an impressive sight, transforming a workaday freight locomotive into the railway equivalent of some dashing Crimean War cavalry officer.

The documentary film, one of several JB made on railways for the BBC and the British Transport

Commission including *John Betjeman Goes by Train* (1962) and *Metroland* (1973), was broadcast on 21st February 1964. The S&D had less than two years to go. Even today, it seems hard to believe that crowded twelve-coach holiday trains, headed perhaps by *Evening Star*, a powerful and speedy 9F 2–10–0, and the very last steam locomotive to be built by British Railways, at Swindon in 1960, once thundered over the green roller-coaster of the Mendips and along a trackbed that seems as remote in many parts now as it would have to those Victorian speculators, and engineers, who so ardently believed that Evercreech and Highbridge would one day be spoken of in railway circles in the same respectful breath as Swindon or Crewe.

4. 'The jolly old train at Rye'

TO GEORGE, ANNE AND ANTHONY BARNES

8th January 1946

Windygates
Songster's Way
Sidcup
Kent

Dear Stuart, Doris and Norman,

Howard and I did very much as you supposed we would, we caught the jolly old train at Rye and changed at Ashford and again at Tub's Hill and Howard couldn't see a tree at Pett's Wood nor could I. Such a pity, it was such unspoiled country before the riff raff came there. Then we changed at Orpington and I just had a sec to pop down to the Estate Agents on the corner of Station road and then it was the eleven eighteen to Penge East through quiet countryside parts until Bickley, where it became all those ugly old grey brick houses – so suburban I think, compared with the sun traps of today – and at Penge East we were quite in a wilderness – *miles* from Crystal Palace Low Level Station so it was bus, bus, bus, trolley

41

bus, bus before we got to old Mr Comper's. The old bird
– Howard says he is early Victorian, positively. Howard
and he talked architecture nineteen to the dozen until
I got heartily sick. Then we went up to the old man's
house on Beulah Hill. Such a funny house, my dears,
all sort of Tudor but not the *real* thing, you know, like they
build nowadays, but in *plaster*, did you ever? and perfectly
enormous and full of stained glass of what Howard says
is a very bad period – 1836 – too late to be real Regency,
which I think divine – Regency I mean. He lives there all
alone and has a garden eleven acres down a sort of
precipice and a lake and a wood at the bottom. The silly
old man refused thirty-five thousand for it because he
said it was the last country left between London and
Croydon. Certainly you can see miles from his terrace but
I would rather have had the oodles than the view. There
he and Howard jawed on all about St Alban's Holborn
and those Victorian churches which Howard says are
hopelessly out of date and should be pulled down for
pre-fab designs, as you must have a house for people
first and proper sanitation and things like that before
all this nonsense about entertainment, museums and
religion. But of course Mr Comper is proper Victorian
and doesn't see things like Howard does.

Well we did enjoy ourselves with you, dears, at that
weekend. Howard said he could have wished he could

have converted you to the flat roof and suggests you put one on Prawls. Windygates seemed very lonely when we got back. The girl was out and the sun parlour window had been left open and smashed one of the vita glass panes which Serge Chermayeff gave us for a wedding gift.

I thought those parcels must have cost you something to send and so enclose a little something to cover postage.

That horrid man you had down – Benjamin or some such name – told Howard that if you had as much trouble in changing the P[ostal] O[rder] as Howard had had in getting it, then you would be quits. I don't like that smart kind of so-called humour.

Again thanks *ever* so,

So long, Darenth

In this tongue-in-cheek letter, the Barnes family have become the Stuart, Doris and Norman of JB's teasing imagination, while he has adopted the persona of Darenth, wife of Howard. They are a suburban couple of some pretension, and greater ignorance although they like to think of themselves as smart, knowing and, above all, Modern. This is, of course, JB at his snobbiest, but the letter is still very funny.

Darenth is named after the Darenth Valley, Kent, where the Barnes lived at Prawls, a house at the sonorously named Stone-cum-Ebony. This might sound like a village in Staffordshire or elsewhere in the Black Country, but it is, in fact, a hamlet close to Rye and the Romney Marshes, a curious and delightful English backwater even today, best known for its famous dry-footed sheep and for the Romney Hythe & Dymchurch Railway, a miniature 15-inch gauge main-line steam railway modelled on the London & North Eastern Railway's route up the east coast to Edinburgh from King's Cross.

In 1946, this part of Kent was criss-crossed by rural railway lines, most of them hacked to pieces by Dr Beeching and his infamous axe. So, the fictitious Darenth, and her dreadful husband, Howard, would have found it no trouble at all to get back from a remote corner of Kent to 'Windygates' their modernised home in Sidcup, a Mock Tudor, or 'Joke Oak', London suburb, by train, some steam, others electric. They would, of course, have had to have changed trains several times. It is these changes that allow JB to indulge his love, and microscopic knowledge, of railway timetables, scenery and architecture as the various trains he cites rattle past.

The Rye to Ashford line through Ham Street and Appledore is still happily with us, still passing through green fields and orchards pretty much all the way.

Rye, East Sussex station, 13th September 1950. The locomotive is a class D3 No. 32379. *R C Riley/Transport Treasury*

Sadly, the last of the traditional 'slam door' trains has gone in the last few years and, together with them, opening windows and sliding 'ventilators' in the carriages. As all trains running these lines are now hermetically sealed and air-conditioned, the smell of the Kent countryside is no longer an attraction for passengers. No more summer breezes. Not much fun. JB was not a fan of air-con, nor is anyone else who truly loves English train travel. Nor, of course, was he a fan of the vast 'sun' or 'picture' windows Modern architects began to insist on in the design of new houses from the early 1930s. Towards the end of the letter,

Approaching Appledore station 23rd May 1961. *L R Freeman / Transport Treasury*

'Darenth' tells Stuart, Doris and Norman (names that JB found funny) that one of the 'vita glass panes' in the 'sun parlour window' which 'Serge Chermayeff gave us for a wedding gift' has been smashed while they were away at Prawls.

Chermayeff (1900–96) was a Harrow-educated, Russian interior decorator, ballroom dancer and architect who was famous for his svelte modern designs, whether for Modern houses or BBC studios. He also designed the recently restored, and rather delightful, De La Warr Pavilion at Bexhill-on-Sea, with Erich Mendelsohn, the famous Prussian emigré architect. When JB was Assistant Editor at the *Architectural Review* (1929–35), he fell, for a dizzy moment, under the spell of the bright young Moderns promoted by the influential monthly magazine. He went so far as to become one of the founding members of MARS (Modern Architecture Research Group), yet, soon enough, returned to his Edwardian and Victorian ways and began to think of 100 per cent Moderns like Chermayeff as figures of fun. Chermayeff's 'vita glass' window would have been the equivalent of a triple-glazed, polarised window in one of the super, high-speed, air-conditioned Eurostar trains that scythe through Kent today on their way from London to Paris and back.

Darenth and Howard change at Ashford, now

an 'International' station complete with stern-faced immigration and crop-haired customs officials in short sleeves and grimaces where Eurostar trains occasionally deign to stop. Ashford itself has changed out of all recognition in recent years; an old market town, it is now home to every latest chain store, shopping mall, baseball cap, shell-suit and leisure activity imaginable. It is more New Jersey, and very much more New Labour, than it is old Kent.

Tubs Hill, where Darenth and Howard change trains a second time is close by Sevenoaks. They take the train to Penge East from Orpington through Bickley partly because JB found the name Penge funny, as he did Neasden. (Penge is a funny word: locals, but only those with a sense of humour, call it 'Pen-gay', which sounds a lot posher than ditch-like Penge); yet, this is presumably where JB himself left the train to take trolleybuses (the last London Transport electric trolleybuses ran in 1962) to visit one of his very favourite living architects, Ninian Comper who lived at The Priory, 67 Beulah Hill, Upper Norwood. Comper – later Sir Ninian – had lived here since 1912, and was to do so until his death; he was 96 and still practising as an architect. JB had 'discovered' Comper in 1938, and published an article on this late-flowering Goth in the *Architectural Review* (the 'Archie' to JB – which was also, of course, the abbreviated name of his much-loved teddy bear, Archibald) the following year.

Comper, born in Aberdeen became one of the very last, and one of the very finest Gothic Revivalists. His best church, St Cyprian's Clarence Gate, sited a few piston-strokes from Marylebone station in central London, remains one of the most beautiful, and numinous in Britain. JB loved Comper not least because the old boy despised the architectural profession and all its toadying, whorish ways, always in search of the latest commission, the latest fad and media attention, and, kow-towing to whichever ghastly government

A locomotive of the Romney, Hythe and Dymchurch railway at Hythe, 15th April 1956. *A R Carpenter/Transport Treasury*

happens to be in power. Comper represented so much of what JB loved and wanted to believe in. Darenth and Howard, of course, would prefer to see the area around his Regency home covered in brash new suburban estates sparkling with 'vita glass' windows if there was money to be made from doing so.

JB's spoof letter ends with a joke against himself; he, of course, is 'that horrid man you had down – Benjamin or some such name.' As for Kent, well, a little of its magic survives, and not least the area around the Darenth Valley, and especially the Romney Marshes where the whistles of the glorious little steam expresses of the Romney Hythe & Dymchurch Railway are still there to remind us of a pre-Beeching world in which it was possible to take a train from almost anywhere to nowhere in particular, if not, clearly, to the Regency charms of Beulah Hill, where a handsome red double-deck trolley bus had to do.

5. 'He must have thought I was Frog'

TO ANNE BARNES

9th September 1946

The Old Rectory
Farnborough
Wantage
Berkshire

Dear Anne,

It is hard to know which to thank the more – you, the Commander or Little P – for my happy stay in France. You, I think, did the most difficult things, like buying a ticket at Auxerre, the Commander on the other hand did the *organising*, Little P, as always, supplied the culture.

A terrible thing happened on the train. I found a carriage to myself (there were no firsts, only seconds and thirds) and a ticket collector climbed in as the train was moving. I gave him my first class ticket with some happy little phrases in French and he moved on. *He must have thought I was Frog* – for about twenty minutes later he came back to the compartment, settled himself

51

down with a pipe and talked volubly and amiably to me – I did not understand one word. He left in a huff.

We had a happy time at Trebetherick and I was able to keep up a daily correspondence with Margaret Wintringham. It loosened the emotional strain and crystallised our relationship, if I may coin a few metaphors. We also went over to see Gerald Berners who was staying with Rowse in a small house outside St Austell and near St Just-in-Roseland. Anthony Brest, who came with us, called the house St Queer-in-Rowsland. Rex W[arner] and Ex [Lady Rothschild] have made a great impression on Gerald. I forgot to tell him about Mrs Reggie Warner.

I am happier and sillier than usual and drinking heavily. I would like to go to France again. That Vouvray! Those snails! Oh! It was worth the journey back.

Love to you all, John B

ere is JB writing to 'Doris' again, only this time she is Anne Barnes proper and he is very much himself. JB had just been on holiday in France with the Barneses, and had clearly enjoyed himself. Back in England, the rest of his holiday was spent at Trebetherick, Cornwall (where he died, aged 77, in 1984). The latter half of the letter is taken up with JB's usual social whirl, with names of a famous historian ('Rowse', or A. L. Rowse, 1903–97, who was born in Cornwall), poet and novelist ('Rex', or Rex Warner, 1905–86, author of the curiously engaging, Kafkaesque novel, *The Aerodrome*, 1941) and socialite ('Ex', or Barbara Hutchinson, first wife of Victor Rothschild). What interests the railway buff, though, is his train journey through France. JB was always so very English, despite his surname, that it is hard to imagine him travelling by foreign train. When he does, as this letter shows, it is, of course, an unenjoyable experience. Like all proper Englishmen travelling by themselves, he liked a compartment in a carriage to himself. What could ever be worse than someone else, anyone else, even if they happened to be HM King George VI, the impossibly glamorous screen goddess Vivien Leigh or Ninian Comper, getting into the same compartment? Actually, there were always two things worse than this possibility. The first was someone who dared to speak above the noise of the rhythm of the train. The second was a foreigner.

JB would have been well aware of the cartoons of 'Pont' from the pages of *Punch*. 'Pont' was the pen-name of Graham Laidler (1908–40), who had been a gifted student at the Architectural Association school in Bedford Square, London. Sadly, he was too sickly to take up a career as an architect; in his brief life, however, he made his lasting mark with superbly drawn and very funny cartoons lampooning the British

THE BRITISH CHARACTER–RESERVE

by permission of *Punch*

Character. One of our characteristics was a fear of travelling in company, and especially of travelling on Continental trains. One of Pont's cartoons shows a young man of JB's type doing his best to retain a politely aloof dignity in a train compartment filled to its gunwhales with jabbering, prodding, over-intimate foreigners. Like many young men of his generation and social milieu, JB assumed an abhorrence of 'Abroad', a place that began at Calais and was full of chattering, uncouth and generally absurd aliens. So, when he finally boards a French train, with a first class ticket, of course, he finds himself not only having to travel second, but also silently engaged in a form of pointless and incomprehensible conversation with a garrulous, and moody ticket collector. The latter leaves 'in a huff' after delivering what appears to have been a twenty-minute monologue. JB, maintaining his assumed upper-class English sang-froid (how French is that?), has refused to reply. How, in any case, could one possibly understand a 'Frog'?

In fact, many of the English upper classes spoke French rather well, and many had built handsome villas which JB might well have loved along the south coast of France and especially around Nice and Menton, close to the Italian border. They steamed down from Paris by the prestigious *Train Bleu*.

Castle class 4–6–0 No. 5024 *Carew Castle* gleams in the sunshine at Exeter St David's, 6th August 1955. *W Hermiston/Transport Treasury*

King class No. 6002 *King William IV* passing Swindon, 16th June 1957.
R C Riley/Transport Treasury

Given his gift as a poet, it is a little sad, perhaps, not to hear JB listening more closely to the train itself. French trains of the time sounded very different indeed from those of his beloved Great Western. Where the 'Star', 'Castle' and 'King' class 4–6–0s, designed by Churchward and Collett at Swindon Works, barked loudly as they exited Brunel's great glass terminus at Paddington and stormed, like thunder, with their chocolate-and-cream coloured holiday trains to Cornwall up precipitous Devon banks, the complex Pacific express locomotives of the SNCF, the nationalised French railways, steamed almost

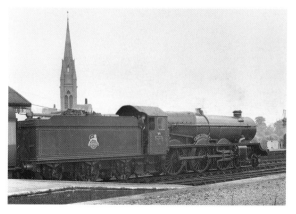

King George V No. 6000, a King class 4–6–0, at Bath Spa station. A very popular locomotive with all steam enthusiasts. *The Ivo Peters Collection*

silently. To JB's eyes, accustomed to the smooth-limbed locomotives of Swindon, the locomotives of André Chapelon, the genius of French steam, would have looked like a mobile exhibition of gratuitous modern plumbing. Ungainly to English eyes, perhaps, these extraordinary locomotives, among the most efficient ever built, pulled away from maritime stations like Calais with a Gallic whisper rather than an Anglo-Saxon yell. They ran uphill and down at a constant speed. Their drivers, men of real learning, were known as 'mécaniciens', or machinists, because they knew the theory as well as the practice of the scientific principles that caused their mounts to steam as smoothly as a crème caramel from one *département* of France to another.

Did all this really pass by JB, a devout steam man and dedicated railway enthusiast? I doubt it. And yet, one always needs to consider to whom it is he is writing. To Anne Barnes, he is the amusing Englishman abroad doing his level best to cope with ridiculous foreign behaviour, rather than a sharp-eyed and keen-eared railway buff. Even so, many railway enthusiasts of JB's generation really did believe that British was best, and even today railway histories written this side of the Channel are almost hilariously chauvinistic. The British did indeed design and build some very fine steam locomotives, and trains for them to pull, yet the most efficient, the most impressive, the most luxurious and the most glamorous locomotives and trains were often to be found elsewhere at the time. If JB had looked hard from his second class train window in the late summer of 1949, he might even have caught a glimpse of SNCF locomotive 242A1, very possibly the finest steam locomotive yet built.

Designed by André Chapelon, this mighty compound 4–8–4 locomotive was almost as powerful as the biggest locomotives in the United States and as

No. 4016 *Somerset Light Infantry, Prince Albert's* near Churston, 5th July 1950. *A Lathey/Transport Treasury*

fast and as efficient as the latest French electrics. She was so good that she was an embarrassment to railway officials in Paris who were set on modernisation, which meant diesel and electric traction on the railways. Shunted off to run the kind of cross-country trains JB suffered in on his French train trip, 242A1 was kept hidden well away from the railway limelight, and scrapped in 1960. There was no French railway equivalent of JB to campaign for her preservation. She had proven that steam really did have a future. Sadly, she was unnoticed by 99.5 per cent of British railway enthusiasts because she was foreign, and, worst of all, French.

6. 'On the way to Marylebone'

8th March 1950

The Old Rectory
Farnborough
Wantage
Berkshire

Dear Mrs Attenborough,

On Central Station I was held up at the barrier by a man looking like this:

I got a closer view of him at the bookstall when he again held me up choosing every daily newspaper. His lips were like this:

and the rest of his face was to scale. He paid for his papers in halfpennies which he counted out one at a time and said to the gal in the bookstall, 'These afepennies are a nuisance to me at pontoon. You can 'ave them.' Then he held me up in the buffet selecting which chemical bun he would have and talking to a choom [sic] as he did so. When the train came in I heard a porter say to him, 'Here you are, Mr Hawkes.' I said to my porter, 'Is that the son of Alderman Hawkes?' He said it was and added,

'The spit of 'is father isn't he.' Thanks to the Principal's vivid story I was able to say 'yes'.

The train grew overheated on the way to Marylebone and we had twice to change engines. I was not surprised.

I *did* enjoy my visit to Leicester and have quite forgotten my terrors before and during the lecture, for delight in the memory of our food, conversation and jokes at your house.

A mad clergyman visited me today and I could not get rid of him until after lunch, so I am rushed for the post.

A thousand thanks for the happy time I had. I enclose a separate and short note of thanks for the Principal to whom the envelope of this letter will be addressed. Come and stay here on your way to the West. It is dirty; but classy-looking outside.

Yours, John Betjeman

JB had lectured at Leicester University and stayed with Mrs and Mr F.L.A., its Principal, and an ardent photographer of churches. David Attenborough, his son, remembered, 'Alderman Hawkes – who was the proprietor of the city's gent's outfitters and who, I'm pretty sure, my father had been trying to extract money from to support the University College and who, I'm equally sure, saw little value in such an institution and had no intention of doing any such thing… .'

Marylebone station in March 1961. Still recognisable.
L R Freeman / Transport Treasury

Nottingham Victoria station in the 1960s. The water pipe in the right foreground has its own brazier for use in winter. *Transport Treasury*

64

JB had given a lecture at Leicester University, and had stayed overnight with the Principal, Frederick Attenborough and his wife, Mary. Two of their three sons have long since been rather famous, Richard, or 'Dickie', the actor and film director, and David, the naturalist, author and broadcaster. JB chose to ride up and down to Leicester from London by the former Great Central Line from Marylebone rather than the Midland from St Pancras. At the time, both lines offered smartly timed services to Leicester. JB's heart, though, was with the GC; it was a more romantic line and enjoyed a fascinating route, climbing out of London and up the Chilterns alongside, and at times on the same tracks as, London Transport's Metropolitan Line. The Met's trains were steam-hauled, until 1961, from Rickmansworth to their – then – terminus at Aylesbury.

The Great Central's London extension down the middle of the country from Nottingham to Marylebone was the last new main line into London until the high-speed Eurostar route through Kent and Essex into St Pancras; services begin running on this line sometime in 2007. The GC reached Marylebone, through Leicester, in 1899. The intention of Sir Edward Watkin, the railway's chairman, was to extend it all the way, via central London and the South Eastern & Chatham

Railway, to Paris through his very own Channel Tunnel. It was a brave dream. Instead of steaming to Paris, from Manchester, the GC terminated in the hallowed quietness of red brick and terracotta Marylebone station. Today, thanks to a great increase in the number of prosperous Chiltern commuters, Marylebone is busier than it ever has been.

Express trains north of Aylesbury, however, ceased running in September 1966. The end had been a long time coming and was very sad. When the GC line was taken over by the London Midland Region of British Railways in the late 1950s, its fate had been sealed. The London Midland favoured the Midland route from St Pancras, and given that there was no room for two main lines competing for the same traffic in the Beeching era, the GC was cruelly pruned, and then axed. I can just remember the last steam-hauled semi-fasts from Marylebone to Leicester Central and Nottingham Victoria. These were only four maroon coaches long, with no buffet, and took forever to get to Nottingham, although the dramatic steam departures through the tunnels under Lord's cricket ground were worth every penny, and it was always a delight to

The Gothic masterpiece – St Pancras station, designed by Sir George Gilbert Scott. Incredibly once threatened with demolition, but saved by the actions of preservationists, including John Betjeman. *Network Rail*

overtake a fast Metropolitan train on adjoining tracks as the 'Britannia' Pacific or 'Black Five' 4–6–0 at the head of the lightweight train galloped down the hill through Neasden and on to the first stop at stream-lined Harrow-on-the-Hill. Sometimes, the London Midland Region management took their policy of putting regular and potential passengers off the GC line to extreme degrees. On one freezing winter's afternoon in 1965, I think it was, one of the semi-fasts to Nottingham left Marylebone behind a Stanier 8F 2–8–0, a freight locomotive not designed to run over 50mph and without provision for steam-heating the two non-corridor coaches that rattled behind it.

Some of the stations on the GC line still exist, including Leicester Central, although this is currently a yard for vans and lorries and a car park. There have been plans to build a marina here, for boats that, somehow, will escape to sea via the local canal system and the River Soar; but, as Leicester is about as far from the ocean waves as any British city, they would, presumably, take even longer to get seaborne than that

Above left: St Pancrnis in 1961 is unrecognisable today as major rebuilding progresses in readiness for the new cross channel link. *J A C Kirke / Transport Treasury*

Left: Leicester station in June 1960. The train is the inaugural service of the Midland Pullman, between London and Manchester. *A Swain / Transport Treasury*

A class V2 2–6–2 No. 60809 *The Snapper, The East Yorkshire Regiment, The Duke of York's Own* at Darlington in July 1955. *A G Ellis / Transport Treasury*

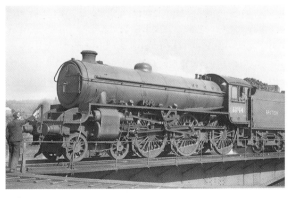

A class B1 4–6–0 No. 61064. *M Robertson / Transport Treasury*

struggling freight locomotive did to get from London to Leicester in the ember days of the old Great Central.

More encouragingly, in recent years, a new, temporary station, Leicester North has been opened. Of no architectural distinction, it nevertheless serves a preserved section of the Great Central from here to Loughborough through the hunting country of the Quorn. This is the one and only double-track preserved steam main-line in Britain, and on a dull and sooty day, it has much of the character of the GC as it would have been in 1950 when JB rode south. I imagine his train composed of a mix of varnished teak coaches built by the former London and North Eastern Railway (which took over the GC in 1923) and perhaps some of the latest 'rhubarb and custard' British Railways standard Mk I coaches. The locomotive, very possibly grimy and a little worse for wear, would have been a Gresley A3 Pacific or V2 2–6–2, or else one of Edward Thompson's purposeful new B1 4–6–0s. The fact that engines were changed twice on the way down to London – little more than 100 miles south – suggests that standards of maintenance were still very much in the doldrums that followed in the wake of the Second World War.

One of JB's fellow passengers was Mr Hawkes Jr, the son of Alderman Hawkes, proprietor of one of

Leicester's leading gents' outfitters. JB pictures him in this letter. It is all rather odd, and not exactly funny. Just why does JB take so very much against the young Mr Hawkes? I have my suspicions. In any case, JB, who lampoons Hawkes in the letter for queuing for tea and a 'chemical bun' appears to have been doing exactly the same.

A class A3 4–6–2 No. 60037 *Hyperion*. The most famous of the A3s, now No. 4472, *Flying Scotsman* is preserved and much used on special excursion trains. *W Hermiston/Transport Treasury*

7. 'Some fascinating cross country route'

TO PATRICK CULLINAN

3rd April 1950

The Old Rectory
Farnborough
Wantage
Berkshire

Dear Patrick,

I will meet you at Newbury Station on Thursday next April 16 at 7.10 p.m. *Unless I hear to the contrary.* There is a train which leaves Paddington at 6 p.m. has Newbury for its first stop.

A really clever boy (which of course you are) would work out some fascinating cross country route in *Bradshaw* e.g. this: Depart Chichester 3.02 p.m. Arrive Fratton 3.27 depart Fratton 3.40 arrive Eastleigh 4.28 (here I have a delicious cup of Southern Region tea in the Refreshment room) depart Eastleigh 5.13 arrive Newbury 6.40. You would by that obscure route avoid the Easter holiday rushes, as few people are clever enough to use any but obvious express trains and they

avoid side lines. Anyhow whether you arrive at
Newbury at 6.40 or 7.10 I will be there at about 7.05.
Much look forward to seeing you. My aged father-in-law
is staying with us and you will cheer us up. He was at
Ladysmith or Mafeking or both or neither. Sorry about
your 'flu. The picture was of Hans Andersen.

 Yours, John Betjeman

JB was one of the greatest *Bradshaw* (railway timetable) enthusiasts and there
was nothing he enjoyed more than being asked how to get from Grimsby to
Sidmouth or some such complicated journey.

Patrick Cullinan (born 1932) is a highly regarded South African poet, born in
Pretoria, who has also been a farmer, publisher, university lecturer and novelist.
He came to England as a young man, and corresponded with JB who recom-
mended that he read Swinburne 'for rhythm', Moore's *Irish Melodies* 'for
ingenuity', and Tennyson 'for variety'. On April 16th 1950, the eighteen-year-
old Cullinan took the train to Newbury to visit JB at Farnborough. Doubtless,
he took the 6pm direct from Paddington, with Newbury its first stop as JB says
in this letter.

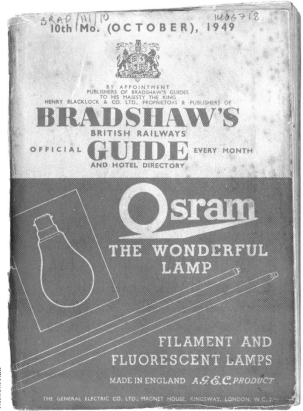

Saturdays only

Saturdays excepted

Saturdays excepted

Saturdays only

Saturdays only

Saturdays Excepted

Saturdays only

Saturdays only

Saturdays excepted

Saturdays only

Saturdays excepted

Saturdays only

Three Bridges (above) dep.
Crawley
Ifield
Faygate
Littlehaven Halt
Horsham
Itchingfield
Dorking North **M**
Warnham
Horsham
Christ's Hospital
Billingshurst
Pulborough
Amberley
Arundel
Ford
Holland Road Halt
Hove
Aldrington Halt
Portslade and West Hove
Southwick
Shoreham-by-Sea **K**
Lancing
East Worthing Halt
Worthing Central
West Worthing
Durrington-on-Sea
Goring-by-Sea
Angmering
Ford (Sussex)
Littlehampton arr.
Littlehampton dep.
Ford (Sussex)
Barnham
Bognor Regis arr.
Bognor Regis dep.
Barnham
Chichester **K**
Fishbourne Halt
Bosham
Nutbourne Halt
Southbourne Halt
Emsworth
Warblington Halt
Havant
Langston Halt
Hayling Island arr.
Havant
Bedhampton Halt
Fratton
Portsmouth & Southsea arr.
Portsmouth Harbour arr.

g Arr. 2 mins. earlier.   *s* Dep. 12 47 p.m. on Saturdays   **For Other Notes, see page 219**

Table 73—continued   PORTSMOUTH, GOSPORT, FAREHAM, SOUTHAMPTON, ANDOVER, and SALISBURY

Week Days—continued

Through Train, Portsmouth and Southsea to Cardiff, page 47

From Fawley dep 3 16 p.m. (Tables 72 and 45)

Through Train, Portsmouth and Southsea to Reading, pages 320 and 43

From Weymouth dep 2 20 p.m. (Table 45)

Saturdays excepted

Through Train to Cheltenham Spa (Lansdown) arr. 8 30 p.m., page 94a

Through Train Portsmouth Harbour to Wolverhampton, arr. 8 57 p.m. pages 320, 43 and 719

Commences 31st May, 1952

Saturdays only

Through Train, Portsmouth and Southsea to Reading, pages 320 and 43

Through Train, Portsmouth and Southsea to Bristol, page 47

To Alton arr. 3 47 p.m. (Table 71)

To Bournemouth West arr 2 52 p.m. (Table 45)

Saturdays only

To Bournemouth West, arr. 9 48 p.m. (Table 45)

To Alton arr. 7 46 p.m. (Table 71)

Z Stops to set down only

SX or SX Saturdays excepted
TH Thursdays only

SO or SO Saturdays only

SO p.m.

A Station for Bishopstoke
B Change at Fratton
E From the Docks and Pier

34	Bognor
	Portsmouth Harbour dep
	Portsmouth & Southsea
	Fratton
	Hilsea Halt
	Cosham
	Portchester
	Fareham arr
	Gosport dep
	Fort Brockhurst
	Fareham arr
	Fareham dep
	Knowle Halt
	Botley
	Swanwick
	Bursledon
	Hamble Halt
	Netley
	Sholing
	Woolston
	Bitterne
	St. Denys
	Southampton Ter (for Docks)
	Southampton Central B
	Millbrook
	Redbridge
	Nursling
	Eastleigh A
	Chandlers Ford
	Romsey
	Mottisfont
	Horsebridge
	Stockbridge
	Fullerton
	Clatford
	Andover Town
	Andover Junction arr
	Grateley
	Porton
	Dean
	Salisbury arr
49	Exmouth (via) dep
50	Lymington
58	Portsmouth (Friary)

Table 64 DIDCOT, NEWBURY, WINCHESTER, and SOUTHAMPTON TERMINUS

Miles		Week Days										Suns.	
		a.m	a.m		a.m	a.m.	a.m		p.m	p.m		p.m	
	61 London (Pad.).... dep	..	5 30	..	9 15	10 45	11 20	..	1 45	4 15	..	1 20	..
	152Oxford .... "	..	7 10	..	10 0	11 15	1 25	..	2 56	5 0	..	1 55	..
—	Didcot.............. dep	..	7 37	..	1050	12 42	2 0	..	3 35	5 52	..	3 0	..
3	Upton and Blewbury....	..	7 45	..	1057	12 49	2 7	..	3 42	6 0	..	3 8	..
6¾	Churn	..	7 52	..	Aa	Aa	Aa	..	Aa	Aa	..	..	..
8¼	Compton	..	7 58	..	11 9	1 0	2 18	..	3 53	6 12	..	3 21	..
10¼	Hampstead Norris.......	..	8 3	..	1115	1 5	2 25	..	3 58	6 18	..	3 27	..
12¼	Pinewood Halt..........	..	8 9	..	1121	1 11	2 31	..	4 4	6 26	..	3 33	..
13¼	Hermitage..............	..	8 12	..	1125	1 14	2 34	..	4 7	6 30	..	3 37	..
18	Newbury............ arr	..	8 20	..	1133	1 25	2 45	..	4 15	6 41	..	3 45	..
—	67 London (Pad.).... dep	..	7 30	..	1045	12 30	..	..	2 35	6 0	..	..	..
—	Newbury........... dep	7 45	9 7	..	1225	2 0	Saturdays only	..	4 32	7 14	..	..	..
21¼	Woodhay	7 52	9 15	..	1232	2 8		..	4 39	7 21	..	..	..
23¾	Highclere..............	7 58	9 21	..	1238	2 14		..	4 44	7 27	..	..	..
25¾	Burghclere	8 3	9 26	..	1243	2 19		..	4 49	7 32	..	..	..
28	Litchfield (Hants.)......	8 9	9 32	..	1249	2 25		..	4 55	7 38	..	..	..
31¼	Whitchurch Town.......	8 17	9 40	..	1257	2 34		..	5 3	7 47	..	..	..
37¼	Sutton Scotney.........	8‖34	9 51	..	1 8	2 46		..	5 14	7 59	..	..	..
40¼	Worthy Down Halt.....	8 42	9 58	..	1 15	2 57		..	5 20	8 6	..	..	..
42¾	King's Worthy..........	8 47	10 3	..	1 20	3 2		..	5 25	8 11	..	..	..
44¼	Winchester C.... arr	8 52	10 8	..	1 25	3 7		..	5 31	8 16	..	..	..
	Winchester C.... dep	9 0	1012	..	1 26	3 22		..	5 38	8 23	..	..	..
47¼	Shawford D.............	9 9	1021	..	1 34	3 29	..	..	5 47	8 32	..	..	..
51¼	Eastleigh F.............	9 17	1028	..	1 41	3 37	..	..	5 54	8 39		..	..
53¾	Swaythling	..	1035	..	2 10	3 46	..	..	6 7	8 47	..	..	..
55	St. Denys	9 25	1039	..	2 15	3 50	..	..	6 11	8 51	..	..	..
56	Northam	..	1043	..	2 19	3 54	..	..	6 15	8 55	..	..	..
56¾	Southampton G.... arr	9 31	1047	..	2 23	3 58	..	..	6 19	8 59	..	..	..

Miles		Week Days											Suns.	
	Terminus	a.m	a.m	a.m	a.m	a.m	p.m	p.m	p.m	p.m	p.m	p.m	p.m	
	Southampton...... dep	..	..	7 22	9 36	1145	..	1 55	..	4 56	..	7 40	..	..
	Northam	..	..	7 35	9 39	1148	..	1 58	..	4 59	..	7 43	..	..
1¼	St. Denys..............	..	..	7 39	9 43	1152	..	2 2	..	5 3	..	7 48	..	..
3¼	Swaythling	..	..	7 43	9 47	1156	..	2 6	..	5 7	..	7 51	..	..
6¼	Eastleigh F............	..	..	7 51	9 56	12 6	..	2 20	..	5 13	..	7 58	..	..
9¼	Shawford D............	..	..	8 0	10 4	1215	..	2 29		5 21	..	8 6	..	..
12½	Winchester C.... arr	..	..	8 8	1012	1223	..	2 37		5 29	..	8 14	..	..
	Winchester C.... dep	..	7 15	8 14	1025	1225	..	2 43	Saturdays only	5 33	..	..	..	..
14¼	King's Worthy	..	7 20	8 21	1030	1231	..	2 50		5 39	..	..	..	..
16½	Worthy Down Halt.....	..	7 26	8 27	1036	1237	..	2 56		5 45	..	..	..	..
19½	Sutton Scotney	..	7 33	8 35	1043	1244	..	3 3		5 52	..	..	..	..
25	Whitchurch Town......	..	7 44	8 46	1055	1255	..	3 14		6 3	..	..	..	..
28¼	Litchfield (Hants.)......	..	7 53	8 55	11 4	1 7	..	3 23		6 12	..	..	..	..
31¼	Burghclere	..	8K3	9 1	1110	1 12	..	3 29		6 18	..	..	..	..
33¼	Highclere..............	..	8 9	9 6	1115	1 17	..	3 35		6 23	..	..	..	..
35¼	Woodhay	..	8 15	9 14	1122	1 22	..	3 42		6 28	..	..	..	..
38¼	Newbury........... arr	..	8 23	9 22	1135	1 30	..	3 55		6 41	..	..	..	..
91½	62 London (Pad.).... arr	..	1015	1115	1 15	3 35	..	5 50	..	8 35	..	..	..	..
—	Newbury........... dep	6 45	..	9 35	..	..	1 58	4 23	5 35	..	7 20	..	8 10	..
43½	Hermitage..............	6 55	..	9 45	..	..	2 7	4 32	5 44	..	7 30	..	8 20	..
44	Pinewood Halt..........	6 58	..	9 48	..	..	2 10	4 35	5 47	..	7 33	..	8 24	..
46¼	Hampstead Norris......	7 3	..	9 54	..	..	2 16	4 41	5 53	..	7 39	..	8 33	..
48¼	Compton	7 12	..	10 0	..	..	2 21	4 47	5 59	..	7 44	..	8 42	..
50	Churn	..	..	Kk	..	..	Kk	Kk	Kk	..	Kk	..	..	..
53½	Upton and Blewbury....	7 22	..	1014	..	..	2 32	4 58	6 9	..	7 54	..	8 53	..
56¼	Didcot.............. arr	7 28	..	1020	..	..	2 38	5 5	6 15	..	8 0	..	9 0	..
67	152Oxford .... arr	8 23	..	11 3	..	..	3 15	5 45	7 12	..	9 15	..	9 32	..
110	61 London (Pad.).... "	9 10	..	1221	..	..	5 33	7 20	7 45	..	9 30	..	1025	..

Aa Stops to take up or set down on previous notice to Station Master at Didcot. Evening trains call during daylight only

C Chesil; about 1 mile to Winchester City Station

D Station for Twyford (Hants)

F Station for Bishopstoke

G Terminus Station for Docks

‖ Arr. 8 28 a.m.

K Arr. 7 59 a.m.

Kk Stops to take up or set down on previous notice to Station Master at Newbury. Evening trains call during daylight only

‡ Third class only

OTHER TRAINS

BETWEEN	PAGE
Winchester and Southampton Terminus	310

Table 65 NEWBURY, BOXFORD, and LAMBOURN—(Third class only)

Miles		Week Days only							
		a.m	a.m		p.m	p.m	p.m	p.m	S
	Newbury............ dep	9 25	1145	..	2 0	4 15	5 12	7 25	1015
¾	Newbury, West Fields..	9 28	1148	..	2 3	4 18	5 15	7 28	..
1½	Speen B............[Halt	9 31	1151	..	2 6	4 21	5 18	7 31	1021
2¾	Stockcross and Bagnor	9 35	1155	..	2 10	4 25	5 22	7 35	1025
4¼	Boxford ....[Halt	9 40	12 0	..	2 15	4 30	5 27	7 40	1030
6¼	Welford Park	9 46	12 6	..	2 21	4 36	5 33	7 46	1036
8¼	Great Shefford..........	9 52	1212	..	2 27	4 42	5 39	7 52	1042
10	East Garston............	9 57	1217	..	2 32	4 47	5 44	7 57	1047
11	Eastbury Halt...........	10 1	1221	..	2 36	4 51	5 48	8 1	1051
12¼	Lambourn.......... arr	10 5	1225	..	2 40	4 55	5 52	8 5	1055

Miles		Week Days only							
		a.m	a.m		p.m	p.m	p.m	S	
	Lambourn......... dep	8 0	1040	..	1240	3 10	6 5	8 45	..
1¼	Eastbury Halt..........	8 3	1044	..	1244	3 14	6 9	8 49	..
2¼	East Garston...........	8 8	1048	..	1248	3 18	6 14	8 53	..
4¼	Great Shefford..........	8 14	1053	..	1253	3 23	6 20	8 58	..
6¼	Welford Park	8 22	11 0	..	1 0	3 30	6 28	9 5	..
7¼	Boxford ....[Halt	8 27	11 5	..	1 5	3 35	6 33	9 10	..
9¼	Stockcross and Bagnor	8 33	1112	..	1 12	3 42	6 39	9 17	..
10½	Speen B...........[Halt	8 37	1115	..	1 15	3 45	6 43	9 20	..
11¼	Newbury, West Fields	8 41	1118	..	1 18	3 48	6 47	9 23	..
12¼	Newbury......... arr	8 45	1120	..	1 20	3 50	6 50	9 25	..

B Station for Donnington. S Saturdays only.

On Sundays, Bus services depart Newbury Station 3 55 p.m. to Lambourn Square: returning from Lambourn Square at 5 50 p.m., by Newbury and District Motor Services Ltd.

Passengers holding rail tickets to Stations and Halts between Newbury and Lambourn inclusive may travel by these Road services without additional charge

At that time, trains along the old Great Western lines had yet to get back up to speed. The Second World War had exhausted Britain's railways, and there were still a few years to go before the glorious 'Kings' and 'Castles', the pride of the GW tracks, were able to run at mile-a-minute timings once again and to speed up to 100mph and more. Young Cullinan's train would have accelerated gently along Brunel's magnificently engineered main-line from Paddington, at first alongside the red electric trains of London Transport's Hammersmith & City line, along past Old Oak Common locomotive depot, through Ealing – Queen of the Suburbs – at sixty and out through Slough, upon which many bombs had fallen during the Blitz, and so on to Reading, with its beer, seeds and biscuits, and out, now cantering along the fringes of the Vale of the White Horse. There would been tinny-tasting tea and curly white bread sandwiches available from the buffet car, cinders raining through the ventilators on Formica-topped tables, and the smell of shoulder-to-shoulder Utility-era English clothing mingled with that of Craven As and Player's Weights. Trains at this time were invariably packed. And, for all the pleasure of riding behind a four-cylinder 'Castle', although the locomotive might have been a less stately 'Hall' designed for 'mixed traffic' rather than expresses alone, Cullinan would probably have been grateful to have alighted at 7.10pm at Newbury. Passengers – known by the latest privatised generation of get-rich-kwik, call centre-style railway management as 'customers' – always 'alighted' from trains at stations (now known as 'station stops' or, if you listen to the BBC or read the *Guardian*, as American-style 'train stations'). Signs on Underground carriages (known as 'cars' from as early as 1900 because they were based on American prototypes) used to warn 'Do Not Alight from Moving Train' for many years. Today, few of the 'customers' eating their delicious combined breakfast-dinner-lunch-teas from disposable polystyrene containers would know what the word means; it is as obscure today as the product names in so many Betjeman poems.

Top right: Hall class 4–6–0 No. 4962 *Ragley Hall* at Newbury, 5th March 1960. *R C Riley / Transport Treasury*

Right: A class M7 0–4–4 T No. 30028 at Alton on the Mid-Hants Railway, en route to Eastleigh, 5th October 1957. *L R Freeman / Transport Treasury*

Chichester station, 29th June 1950. *R C Riley / Transport Treasury*

King class 4–6–0 No. 6004 *King George III* at Paddington station.
Transport Treasury

8. 'From Oxford by train'

TO LADY MANDER

14th March 1950

The Old Rectory
Farnborough
Wantage
Berkshire

Dear Lady Mander,

I am sorry to be so long in answering your nice letter of March 6th. I have been away until this morning and no letters forwarded.

I shall be coming from Oxford by train reaching Wolverhampton Great Western Station at five forty-five (DV) on Friday. Alas, I shall have to return by the ten twenty on Saturday morning. It is most annoying, but I have a luncheon engagement near here which I cannot avoid.

I want to see as much as possible of what you think I ought to see. Most exciting of all will be Wightwick. I have been reading the guide book you sent to me. It sounds like the very best of Kempe. I suppose Grayson, of Grayson and Ould, is the man who did 'High Meadow' Claughton, Cheshire and the City Liberal Club, Walbrook, and competed unsuccessfully for Brompton Oratory. I look forward to seeing Wolverhampton and the theatre you mention if there is a chance of getting into it before catching the ten twenty in the morning. There is so much to see and so much to do and so little life to do it in. Oh dear, I *am* excited!

Alas, Penelope is away until after I leave for Wolverhampton. She is in retreat for Lent. So it will only be me, the tired old prima-donna of the early thirties.

Yours sincerely, John Betjeman

Here, JB is in a hurry again, just as he was when asked down to Alresford by John Arlott. He is planning to ride up by train to visit Lady Mander who lives at Wightwick Manor, the gloriously theatrical Arts and Crafts mansion near Wolverhampton built for her family, who had been wealthy paint manufacturers and suppliers. Completed in 1887 to the designs of Edward Ould, and extended considerably in 1893, Wightwick was a showcase of original William Morris wallpaper, De Morgan tiles, Pre-Raphaelite paintings and stained glass by Charles Kempe. How could JB possibly have refused an invitation? The house had, in fact, been handed over to the National Trust as early as 1937 by Sir Geoffrey Mander MP, and so it was open to the public, although the Manders maintained a wing of the house, and continue to do so today.

Sir Geoffrey had tried to sell the house from 1926, but no one was interested. Writing in the local newspaper, the *Express and Star*, in September 2003, Anthea Mander said that, 'At first the National Trust were reluctant to take it, but people like John Betjeman said one day people would be interested in the Victorian era and how right they were. My memories of it are that it was very lonely and cold … and I have never got over those things. You are very isolated and you don't have neighbours. Also there was nowhere you could bring somebody home, there, nowhere to go.' Despite the immense scale and sprawl of Wightwick, Mrs Mander said that 'in reality, only the library and the nursery were used.' Looking at the ambitious plans of the vast houses commissioned by rich late Victorian entrepreneurs, this was probably true of very many of them. This would also help to explain why it was always going to be harder for JB and his peers to save Victorian houses than it was their Georgian predecessors; the latter were mostly much smaller and much easier to live in. Great Victorian houses, like great Victorian steam locomotives, required relays of servants to keep them running.

This letter displays JB's wonderfully arcane, and intimate, knowledge of such late nineteenth-century English architecture. I like the way he casually mentions Grayson's, of Grayson and Ould, unsuccessful competition entry for the design of Brompton Oratory. He really did have an encyclopaedic mind for this kind of Victorian detail, just as he knew his *Bradshaw* and the classes of Great Western locomotives.

The run from Oxford up to Wolverhampton would have been a quick and easy one even in 1950. The station at Oxford, a pretty dismal thing then, is truly horrid today. It does seem odd that this gateway

Castle class 4–6–0 No. 5038 *Morlais Castle*, 14th August 1957.
J Robertson / Transport Treasury

to Oxford has always been third class. Quite why is a mystery far deeper than any Dan Brown might dream up. The trains, though, were handsome things at the time of JB's trip. A rake of chocolate and cream coaches, perhaps, would, in all probability, have been whipped up to Banbury, Birmingham and Wolverhampton behind one of Charles Collett's peerless 'Castle' class 4–6–0s. Built from 1923 to 1950, these handsome, strong, economical locomotives were also fleet of foot. In fact in their later years with British Railways, they were often steamed up to 100mph and more, and hold the record for the fastest average speed ever for a steam run on the British main line. This was between Swindon and Paddington, at 81.6mph.

Named after British castles, these locomotives were designed and built to the highest specifications; they

were, I suppose, the railways' equivalent of Arts and Crafts architecture, appearing to be old fashioned, and yet built using the best mix of new and old materials and know-how. The 1893 extension of Wightwick Manor was made using a new-fangled steel frame; although it would be impossible to guess, the house is much more modern in structural terms than many of the Modern Movement houses built in Britain in the 1930s when JB was a member of the Modern Architecture Research Group.

'Castles' were much the same. Although they always had something of a Victorian air about them, their workings were developed and improved right up until the late 1950s and were always up to the mark no matter what was demanded of them. The last ran, in regular British Railways' service, from Paddington to Banbury in June 1965. Of course, it is just possible that JB might have ridden up to Birmingham behind a Great Western 'Star', precursor of the 'Castle' and designed by one of the world's great locomotive engineers, George Jackson Churchward. He died, in retirement but was unable to keep away from Swindon Works and was killed when one of his own

A Star class 4–6–0 No. 4030 with the *Cornishman* approaches Plymouth North End station, 22nd June 1953. *A Lathey/Transport Treasury* locomotives at the head of an express train ran him down as he tried to cross the tracks close to his Swindon home, 'Newburn.' JB would have known that story. Although in a hurry, I'm sure he enjoyed the excuse to ride the train to Wolverhampton just as much as he did the eccentric and over-ambitious architectural pleasures of Wightwick Manor.

9. 'At Uffington oil-lit station'

TO ENDELLION LYCETT GREEN

21st July 1977

29 Radnor Walk
London SW1

Darling Delli,

That was a very nice long letter you sent to me and so in return I am going to tell you a long, quite true story which happened to me and I wonder what you can make of it.

When Gramelope and I were just married, we lived in a farmhouse in Uffington, Berkshire in the Vale of the White Horse. We lived there because it was the furthest place from London I could find which you could leave and get back to in a day. Fares were low, it was lovely getting beyond Reading in the train from London into what was true country. In Uffington people still talked with Berkshire accents like Pam Ayres on the television. A lot of them were called Ayres and must have been her relations. Uffington had its own railway station then lit with oil lamps. It was a junction for Faringdon and a little train left on a single line from Uffington station through fields to a terminus some way out of the town of Faringdon. Many people from Uffington had never been to London. Swindon was the other big town near us.

I used to get up at about seven in the morning and Gramelope would drive our car to Uffington or Challow Station (both of them are now shut) and there at about 7.30 I would catch a slow train to Didcot and then a fast one to London. I was working on the *Evening Standard* newspaper in those days writing about new films. We used to be shown the films in the morning and I would have to write about them in the afternoon and then catch the train home. It was always a bit of a rush. The slowest part of the journey was the underground railway from Paddington to Farringdon Street, the nearest underground station to the *Evening Standard* office.

I remember how glad I used to be in the evenings to get back to Berkshire. The further we were from London, the quieter everything grew. Gramelope had a white Arab horse called Moti and she used to meet me at Uffington oil-lit station and we were very happy to be in real country and alone.

One morning I was travelling down on the Inner Circle underground from Paddington to Farringdon Street when the train did a very unusual thing. It waited for a long time at King's Cross station. My father, your great-grandfather, had a factory, founded in 1820, on the Pentonville Road (it is still there and now owned by the Medici Society). King's Cross underground was the nearest station. I remember thinking as the train waited at King's Cross, 'Shall I go out and see my father?' A voice inside me seemed to say, 'Yes, do go and see him. It won't take you long and you won't be too late for the film.' The train went on waiting but I felt too lazy at that time of the morning to bother to get out and take a tram up the hill. Then we went on and with other film writers I saw an American musical film called *George White's Scandals*.

When I got back to Uffington that evening the telephone rang. It was my father's managing clerk, Mr H. V. Andrew, and he told me that my father had died that morning while talking to him. He was recalling a date. Do you think my father was trying to get through to me? Do you think he knew he was going to die so swiftly? I don't know. All I can tell you is that it happened and Gramelope will remember it.

She offered me a strawberry that we had grown in our garden at Uffington when I heard the news and I remember being too upset to want to eat it. This is the longest letter I have written to you and it is in return for yours to me. It is the only ghostly experience I had which can be witnessed.

I enclose a silver Maria Theresa dollar. These are specially made at the Mint for Arab countries which will use no other currency.

Love from Grandpapa

Uffington station, 26th April 1959 with Castle class 4–6–0 No. 5016 *Montgomery Castle* passing through. *R C Riley/Transport Treasury*

This lyrical letter is addressed to JB's granddaughter, Endellion Lycett Green. JB speaks fondly of Uffington and Challow stations in the Vale of the White Horse on the old Great Western mainline between Didcot and Swindon. Sadly, these stations have long closed and passengers on today's thirty-year-old turbo-charged HSTs (High Speed Trains) galloping to and from London, Bristol and the West Country would be hard-pressed to pinpoint these 'oil-lit' stations. Today's commuters must drive to either Swindon or Didcot to catch trains east and west, while many probably think 'what the hell' and drive all the way to their destination along the relentlessly boring M4.

And, yet, perhaps because the stations have been closed for so very long, and because the motorway roars past unheeding, the landscape of the Vale of the White Horse has escaped much of the cynical, or uncaring, modern development all too evident in and around Swindon, and, increasingly, Didcot.

Didcot itself remains a railway enthusiast's oasis. It is home to the Great Western Society and its engine shed, in the long shadow of the handsome cooling towers of Didcot Power Station designed by Sir Frederick Gibberd, architect of 'Paddy's Wigwam' – Liverpool's 1960s' Roman Catholic cathedral. As for

Swindon, although it has a shiny new museum dedicated to the history of the Great Western Railway, the historic locomotive workshops themselves are now a 'designer retail outlet' – yet another shopping mall. With the exception of one or two steam specials, privatised and shopaholic Britain is no longer able to build railway locomotives.

The former branch from Uffington to Faringdon nosing towards the Thames Valley seems very remote indeed today. The remoteness of the area when the Betjemans came to live here in the 1930s is well attested by JB when he writes 'Many people from Uffington had never been to London.' And, instead of pan-Southern English BBC-style 'mockney', local people 'still talked with Berkshire accents like Pam Ayres', a poet as popular in her own way as Betjeman. In June 2006, Pam Ayres unveiled a plaque at the house where JB and Penelope once lived in Uffington.

The contrast between life on the news desk at the *Evening Standard* and country life in and around Uffington, Berks, must have been as wide as the big screens on which JB watched the latest Hollywood and home-grown films before rattling off his reviews and catching the train back from Paddington. JB did not last very long as a film critic. To amuse himself, he would ask the latest Hollywood or Elstree starlets for their preferences as regards the various styles of English Gothic architecture, and write up their absurd answers.

The slowest part of his journey through those pre-war White Horse years, he writes, was 'the underground railway from Paddington to Farringdon Street.' Sometimes, nothing changes. That stretch of line – the world's first underground railway, opened in 1863 – is as slow today as it would have been in JB's *Evening Standard* days. But there have been changes, of course. Remarkably, when JB came this way, Pullman car trains still rumbled between Baker Street and through Farringdon (the 'Street' has since been dropped from the station name) to Liverpool Street, and thus the plutocratic banks of the City of London. The Pullman cars – there were two of them on the Metropolitan Line named *Mayflower* and *Galatea* – continued to run out to Aylesbury until the outbreak of the Second World War. Today, of course, there is no need for such dining cars on the Underground: every car is a buffet car, with aromatic take-away meals consumed at every seat and tss-tss-tss music provided by hundreds of insistent 'personal' stereos. Dress code for the Underground: American kindergarten. Language: Anglo-Saxon.

Trains running – probably the wrong word – along this line stop below where once the Euston Arch used

The magnificent arch at Euston station that JB failed to save.
Lucas/Transport Treasury

to be. JB failed to save this wonderfully grandiloquent Grecian gateway (designed by Philip Hardwick, 1792–1870) to what had been the original London and Birmingham Railway station opened here in 1837. The trains also stop, more happily at Kings Cross–St Pancras. Both these Victorian stations are now in safe hands; both are being thoroughly restored. St Pancras, all Gormenghast Gothic prickles and brash red Midlands' brick, will be the railway gateway to France and the Continent sometime in 2007. Further down the line is Liverpool Street, a great Early English-style Gothic railway cathedral, saved by JB and other friends of the railways, and rebuilt, happily for the most part, from the late 1980s.

Of all these famous stations, the one that has changed the least is surely Farringdon (Street). This was the eastern, or City, terminus of the original Metropolitan Railway. Of course, there have been rebuilding works years over the past 140 years, yet the station still boasts an overall glass roof, a long-closed 'Parcels' Office', and the air of a station that was once far more important than it is today. For many years JB would have used this station not just for work, but for any number of reasons while he rented a small flat in Cloth Fair, five minutes' walk from the station through Smithfield meat market. Then, as during my childhood in the 1960s and 70s, the entire area beyond the station was almost incredibly old-fashioned. Soot-encrusted. Dripping with blood. Dickensian. As late as 1971, it was possible to hear the beat of Great Western steam locomotives echoing from beneath the glass roof of Farringdon station. Determinedly modern people said we must be hearing ghosts. Far from it; London Transport maintained a small stud of former Great Western 57xx class pannier tank engines at Neasden Depot into the era of wide lapels and Jason King moustaches. It was, though, an extraordinary sight to watch steam locomotives cantering through Underground tunnels late at night, or very early in the morning as the butchers in white medieval hoods from Smithfield market stepped over to the Fox and Hounds for a dawn pint and fry-up.

The area has changed almost out of recognition since. Washed, brushed and even sanitised, Smithfield and the streets winding away from Farringdon Station are home to important young architects and 'cutting-edge' graphic designers today. And to significant bars, critically acclaimed restaurants and all-night thumpa-whompa-thumpa nightclubs from which ghostly pale yoof in kiddy romper gear emerges as the first commuters arrive clutching take-away 'lattes' ('milks' in Italian; pronounced 'lar-tays' in London).

The majestic *King George V* No. 6000, a King class 4–6–0, resplendent in its new BR livery – blue lined out in black and white, 22nd June 1949. *The Ivo Peters Collection*

Kings Cross station, the view north from the roof. *R E Vincent / Transport Treasury*

The ghost JB felt here, while his Metropolitan or Circle Line train stopped at King's Cross, was that of his father. He had long felt guilty for refusing to take on the family furniture and luxury goods business – the building is there still – and now must have felt at least doubly wretched for not seeing his father just before he died, mere yards away from where JB's Underground train stood, held up by signals. Not even the fresh strawberry Penelope offered that evening when he returned to Uffington could console him. It is, though, on train journeys, that we often think of friends, relations, past loves, passions and guilts as the train itself speeds unheedingly along.

10. 'We could all set up at Bodmin Road'

TO PEGGY THOMAS

26th September 1958

43 Cloth Fair
London EC1

Dearest Peggy,

I can hardly believe, in fact I cannot believe, that this day last week Candida and I walked through the mist to the Rumps and saw a seal and that in the evening we went to Pendogget for that Old Harrovian fare and now I am in the heart of London pitying myself so much that I am sweating with self-pity and poor Candida is in Paris trailing round after culture with Paul and Penelope. I keep recalling your remark that Trebetherick is like an unsuccessful love affair, always having to be broken up because of outside hostile circumstances. And perhaps if we really live there for ever, as we long to do, we'll get like Miss Collins, though at the moment I envy the very apples that rot on her garden path and the puniest slug that slides over her threshold. Perhaps we could all set up at Bodmin Road station by arrangement with the Great Western –

you in the refreshment room because of drink, Lynam in the signal box because of administrative ability, me in the booking office because I'm literary, Edward [Hornby] to do the lamps and odd jobs because he's so clever with his hands, Douglas to look after the down platform as head porter and Ted as outside boy, pushing trolleys to Bodmin and meeting motor cars on arrival. We won't have a station master, as we'll be one glorious Soviet. Joan [Kunzer] will run the Bodmin branch.

I always enjoy Cornwall more than anything that happens to me in the year and this year I can say that I enjoyed myself more than ever. My! how we laughed! How marvellous you and Lynam are as hosts, how good Joan and Edward [Mott] and Douglas [Eaves] as company. Dear, sweet Peggy, I can never thank you enough for your kindness and Lynam's kindness to

Yours, Chris Guiney[?]

pp Jan Trebetjeman

P.T. was married to Lynam T., headmaster of Repton School, in whose holiday house, White Horses at Trebetherick, we often stayed.

Miss Collins was a fearsome and eccentric spinster who lived in Trebetherick.

Edward Hornby was a regular guest at White Horses.

Joan Kunzer (née Larkworthy) was JB's earliest girl chum. He had met her at Trebetherick when he was four years old.

Edward Mott was a contemporary of P.T.'s son Michael.

Douglas Eaves had been in Lynam T.'s house at Rugby (before the latter became headmaster of Repton) and had gone on to be a schoolmaster at the Dragon School.

Happily, Bodmin Road station survives, and even thrives, although it has since been renamed Bodmin Parkway in honour of the car. Dr Beeching and various governments of the 1960s and later did their best to close every last railway in Devon and Cornwall. As recently as 2005, the government sought to axe the much loved sleeper train from Paddington through Bodmin Parkway to Penzance. By the summer of the following year, demand for the sleeper was heavier than it had ever been. British governments despise railways and have, over the past forty years, done pretty much everything they have been able to do to undermine and even destroy them. They must not, will not win. Trains will continue to run through and stop at Bodmin Parkway for generations to come, even if the line that gets them there from London, Bristol, Exeter and Plymouth might no longer be able to run alongside the fierce waves that dash against the Great Western coast between Dawlish and Saltash. This sensational line may well be diverted inland in coming years; if not, it is likely to be washed away as the Arctic icecap melts and the levels of the world's seas rise.

Bodmin Road – let's forget 'Parkway' for the moment – resounds to preserved steam trains as well as to Great Western main-line diesels today. The steam trains of the Bodmin and Wenford Railway takes

Bodmin Road station and an early DMU leaving for Penzance, 2nd May 1961. *R C Riley/Transport Treasury*

The *Cornish Riviera Limited* hauled by King class 4–6–0 No 6008 *King James II* near Teignmouth, August 1957. *J Robertson/Transport Treasury*

passengers to Bodmin proper. Bodmin Road, although a very simple station of no particular architectural distinction, remains a delightful spot, and would be a good choice for a 'soviet' of railway-minded writers and others today as it was some half-century ago when JB wrote this letter to Peggy Thomas. Mrs Thomas was the wife of Lynam Thomas, headmaster of Repton School. They owned a house, White Horses, at Trebetherick where the Betjemans often stayed during the summer holidays. JB was back in London, dreaming of Cornwall at the close of the holidays, alone again while Penelope, their son Paul, and daughter, Candida, were 'trailing around after culture' in Paris. Not, though, for JB the lure of the Louvre, nor the Luxembourg Gardens, nor even lunch at the wonderfully atmospheric Train Bleu restaurant – still very much there – at Gare du Nord. He thought instead of Bodmin Road, offering jobs there, in his gently simmering imagination, to old Cornish friends from childhood, like Joan Kunzer, and to fellow guests of the Thomas's at White Horses.

Since then, many main-line stations like Bodmin Road, have lost their staff, their signal boxes, flower beds, Gentlemen's lavatories and Ladies' waiting rooms, too. Bodmin Road is different because the preservationists have arrived and there are plenty of people, at weekends, on holiday or in retirement, who are very happy indeed to act as signalmen, booking office clerks and porters. They enjoy bringing neglected flower beds to life, touching up paintwork, polishing brass and answering passengers' questions knowledgeably.

When JB mentions running Bodmin Road station as a 'soviet', he is, of course, teasing. This was the time when the former Soviet Union and the Cold War was at its height. Perhaps rather curiously, and despite the collapse of the old Communist monster, Russian railways remain some of the world's finest. Long-distance trains are handsome, efficient, on time and generally very friendly. Food is usually freshly cooked in kitchen cars, their staff collecting local produce at stations along the line. There are often fresh flowers in compartments, and tea available, thanks to samovars installed in every carriage, around the clock. It would, presumably, be beyond the wit of the fast-buck, annual-bonus merchants who run trains in Britain today, to think of serving fresh food or having fresh flowers in vases on dining car tables. Imagine strawberries and cream on summer trains through Bodmin Road …

Bodmin Road appealed to JB for a number of reasons. It was one way to summer holidays spent at Trebetherick, although the Betjemans usually went,

The down *Cornishman* express at Teignmouth behind Castle class 4–6–0
No. 5071 *Spitfire*, July 1956. *Transport Treasury*

in JB's childhood, by London & South Western train
from Waterloo via Launceston, alighting at Wadebridge. He liked Bodmin Road, too, because it occupies
a rather idyllic setting close to the River Fowey and
right by Lanhydrock House and its beautiful gardens.
Rebuilt in Victorian Gothic style by the Cornish
architect Richard Coad, this former Augustinian
priory, is an enchanting place. Today, it is owned by the
National Trust, and is one of its most visited proper-
ties. I think, too, that JB would have enjoyed the early
story of Bodmin Road station. Such was the snobbery

concerning railways coming to town – coupled to a real fear of the smoking, snorting train – that local landowners refused to allow tracks into Bodmin itself. So, the broad gauge line was laid some miles to the south, meaning that a branch line would one day have to be built to connect the town to the main-line. When it arrived, the tracks were laid to narrow gauge, meaning that trains from Bodmin could go no further then Bodmin Road. As a result, the junction was much

A gleaming King class 4–6–0 No. 6009 *King Charles II* approaching Exeter St David's, August 1954. *J Robertson/Transport Treasury*

busier than it needed to be, with livestock and agricultural produce changing trains along with passengers. It was only in 1892 that the broad gauge tracks – seven feet and a quarter inches between them – were re-laid, from Penzance to Paddington, with the four feet eight and a half inches of the 'standard gauge.'

JB wrote this letter just as the character of the Great Western lines through Cornwall was about to change for perhaps the first time since the First World War, even taking into account the nationalisation of the railways that had been enacted in 1948. It was in 1958 that the first diesels made their way into the county and that its snaking branch lines came under real threat. Roads through Cornwall, though, were agonisingly slow, and despite the deep-rooted English love of hot, sticky summer traffic jams, trains along the Great Western main lines were very busy indeed. Although they are not quite so special as they were in 1958, today's Great Western trains are equally busy, and, happily, they still serve Bodmin Road, or Parkway, where, much to the surprise of passengers busy eating, text messaging, eating, making vital calls on their mobiles, eating, spreading their legs out as far as possible into the aisles, and eating, steam trains await their arrival across the platform. Sadly, they will not find JB in the booking office.

John Betjeman looks down from the foot plate of Castle class locomotive
Clun Castle. He has adopted the classic pose of the old GWR engine driver
and is enjoying himself at the New England shed, Peterborough, in 1967.
© *R H N Hardy/Transport Treasury*